RAILWAY HISTORY IN PICTURES:
IRELAND Volume 2

A Great Northern S2 class locomotive No 190, **Lugnaquilla**, heading the heavy afternoon 'Mail' from Londonderry to Belfast on the climb up the bank between Carrickmore and Pomeroy, County Tyrone, in June 1952.

The first three carriages are centre-corridor thirds, the fourth a restaurant car, the fifth a steel-framed side-corridor composite, the sixth an eight-wheeled bogie brake, the seventh a steel-framed through carriage from Derry to Dublin, via Portadown, and the eighth a 20 ton parcel van.

RAILWAY HISTORY IN PICTURES

Ireland Volume 2

ALAN McCUTCHEON
MA PhD FSA FRGS

DAVID & CHARLES : NEWTON ABBOT

ISBN 0 7153 4998 8

COPYRIGHT NOTICE

© ALAN McCUTCHEON 1970

All rights reserved. No part of this publication may be reproduced, stored in a retrieval system, or transmitted, in any form or by any means, electronic, mechanical, photocopying, recording or otherwise, without the prior permission of David & Charles (Publishers) Limited

Set in ten on twelve point Plantin
and printed in Great Britain
by W. J. Holman Limited Dawlish
for David & Charles (Publishers) Limited
South Devon House Newton Abbot Devon

CONTENTS

	Page
INTRODUCTION	6
INDUSTRIAL RAILWAYS, INCLUDING CONTRACTORS' LINES	7
TOURIST SERVICES AND BOAT TRAINS	14
COMMUTER SERVICES AND LOCAL TRAINS	26
RAILWAY ARCHITECTURE AND DESIGN AFTER 1870	31
LOCOMOTIVE DEVELOPMENT AFTER 1900	44
SPECIAL SERVICES AND ROYAL TRAINS	53
STEAM CARRIAGES, INSPECTION VEHICLES, RAIL-CARS AND BUSES, ROLLING STOCK	62
HEY-DAY AND DECLINE	71
RECENT DEVELOPMENTS	92
RECORDING AND PRESERVATION	100
ACKNOWLEDGMENTS AND SOURCES	105
BIBLIOGRAPHY	106
INDEX	110

INTRODUCTION

The hey-day of the Irish railway system dates from the years immediately before and after World War I. These years saw the introduction of many important locomotive classes with which services were accelerated throughout the country. In civil engineering and railway construction too, expansion and improvement were still the keynote; minor additions were made to the established networks and substantial schemes of track realignment and improvement were carried out, north and south. Moreover, by 1910 a large number of narrow-gauge railways were operating in Ireland, with varying degrees of commercial success, both as transport systems in their own right and also as 'feeders' by which an extension of rail transport had been possible into the remoter, less densely populated areas of the mountain fringe. As yet there was no alternative means of travel to compete with the comfort and reliability of the steam train, and in the carriage of freight, minerals and agricultural produce its dominance was even more pronounced.

No one could have foreseen the speed and thoroughness with which this position of superiority was to be undermined in the years which followed, mainly of course as a result of the appearance of road vehicles on Irish roads in increasing numbers from the early 1920s. Stung by such competition the railways produced some of their finest workings and fastest schedules during the years 1920-40, a period which provides much of interest to the Irish railway historian, both in locomotive performance and general railway working.

Since 1945 four themes have dominated rail transport in Ireland—amalgamation, dieselisation, closure and preservation—and a period of readjustment and drastic reshaping of services has now been succeeded by one of relative stability.

This book continues the story of Irish railways and brings the reader right up to the present with a consideration of Irish railways as they are today. An attempt is made to place the railways against the environment in which they exist(ed) and to outline the main factors influencing the way in which those which are left appear to be developing. With so much already gone, special attention is given to the problems of study, recording and preservation. While this forms the subject of the final section, however, there is still a large part of the story of Irish railway history to be told and much of this second volume is concerned with special aspects of Irish railway working and with the determined efforts made by the railways to maintain their position over the past fifty years in the face of increasing operational difficulties.

INDUSTRIAL RAILWAYS INCLUDING CONTRACTORS' LINES

Though modest in comparison with the basic role played by rail transport in the development of heavy industry in Great Britain, the uses made of railways, both broad and narrow gauge, in assisting certain specific industrial enterprises in Ireland, or in actively contributing to the construction of certain major works of civil engineering, are not without interest. From the very large number available, ten examples have been selected, representing a wide distribution in space and time.

The Carnlough Limestone Railway was a private system operated by the local limestone company at their quarries on the Antrim coast, overlooking the town and harbour of Carnlough. A cable-operated railway on a 4 ft 8½ in gauge started work in August 1854, linking the quarries in Gortin with the harbour, while a 3 ft 6 in track led from the harbour to quarries in the townland of Tullyaughter, some distance up the valley behind the town. These lines passed over both the main 'Coast Road' and a street running parallel to it a short distance inland. The Tullyaughter line was in all probability worked by horses until the introduction of an 0–4–0T by A. Barclay of Kilmarnock in 1898. The illustration here shows this locomotive, **Otter**, shunting at Carnlough harbour early in the century with a train of full waggons from the Tullyaughter quarries.

The harnessing of the Shannon at Ardnacrusha, near Limerick, to supply electricity to the greater part of the Irish Republic, was a major feat of civil engineering; a gigantic scheme carried out between 1925 and 1930. From Longpavement, north of Limerick, a track laid to a gauge of 900 mm by Siemens Bauunion, a sister company of the main contractors, led through the countryside to O'Briensbridge, with an extensive network of branch lines, some on a gauge of 600 mm, diverging here and there to the various huge excavators and dredgers in use at that time.

Near the end of the contract a 5 ft 3 in branch of the 'Great Southern' system was built from Longpavement to the generating station at Ardnacrusha. For part of its length this line was of mixed gauge, one rail being used by both 900 mm and 5 ft 3 in track. Shown above is a contractor's train running on the 900 mm track at Ardnacrusha, with mixed-gauge track in the foreground.

In the scenic grandeur of the Mourne Mountains in County Down the Silent Valley, above Annalong, was flooded to become the main reservoir for the Belfast area. In the 1920s a complex system of 4 ft 8½ in track was laid down in the area, and from the site of the main dam down to Annalong, by the principal contractors, S. Pearson & Co Ltd; ten locomotives were in use, hauling trains of open waggons. Shown at the foot of page 8 is **Courtney**, an 0–6–0 saddle tank built by the Avonside Engine Co of Bristol in 1912. Like all the other locomotives used here, when the contract was finished the engine was sold to George Cohen & Sons Ltd.

Within the extensive brewery of Arthur Guinness Son & Co Ltd in Dublin, an extensive network of narrow-gauge railways, laid on a gauge of 1 ft 10 in, served the various works sections, while a 5 ft 3 in gauge line led from the brewery across the road to the Kingsbridge terminus of the GS & WR system. To work the internal traffic the brewery's chief engineer, Mr Samuel Geoghegan, designed a most unusual form of locomotive, an 0–4–0T, of which the prototype was built by the Avonside Engine Co in 1882, and a further eighteen by William Spence of Dublin between 1887 and 1921. In these engines the cylinders were situated over the boiler, the drive being transmitted from the crank shaft to the wheels by vertical connecting rods; thus, the motion was kept well away from the ground and dirt, a problem which had bedevilled earlier, more conventional locomotives. The wheels were 1 ft 10 in in diameter, the cylinders 7 in × 8½ in, the boiler pressure was 160 psi and the total weight was 7.4 tons. A point worth noting was the lack of consideration shown for the driver, whose 'footplate' was the coal in the bunker, on which he stood; his balance was maintained by hanging on to the regulator. Moreover, as there are many places in the brewery with low head-room he was often forced to drive in a crouched position to avoid decapitation. These locomotives handled all the internal narrow-gauge traffic until 1947 and no less than five are now preserved in museums in Great Britain and Ireland.

As well as handling the internal narrow-gauge traffic at the brewery, the Geoghegan locomotives coped with the heavy broad-gauge traffic moving to and from Kingsbridge and it was not until 1914 that the first broad-gauge steam locomotive was purchased. The operation of narrow-gauge engines on broad-gauge track was made possible by use of a set of ingenious 'haulage waggons' or bogies in which the narrow-gauge locomotive's driving wheels rested on grooved friction wheels carried by a countershaft, which was geared to drive the bogie at half engine speed. The narrow-gauge locomotive was lifted on to the bogie by a hydraulic hoist, replaced in 1950 by an electric hoist. There were four haulage trucks in all, built by Spence between 1888 and 1903, and right to the end of the broad-gauge line's existence Nos 1 and 4 were in working order.

Here we see haulage trucks Nos 2 and 3 with a narrow-gauge locomotive being raised into position on the hydraulic hoist, and (opposite), narrow-gauge locomotive No 20, now in the Transport Museum in Belfast, on haulage truck No 3 engaged on light shunting work, August 1957.

The line of the British Aluminium Company at Larne Harbour, used for carrying ore from the factory to the quayside, opened in 1900 and closed in 1960. A 3 ft gauge line worked originally by three small tank engines by Peckett & Sons Ltd of Bristol, the Larne line enjoyed the distinction of being the last narrow-gauge railway in County Antrim to use a steam locomotive. Shown here is locomotive No 1, built in 1904, shunting at the Larne quays, with a train of ore waggons. This locomotive is now in private ownership in Ulster.

In 1948 coal sidings were constructed from the Larne branch of the former Belfast & Northern Counties system at Mount, near Carrickfergus, to meet the needs of the giant factory being built on the lough shore by Courtaulds Ltd. Two steam locomotives were acquired, 0–4–0 saddle tanks by Peckett of Bristol, and these remained in use until quite recently, ferrying trains of coal waggons down into the works from the main line. Shown here is **Wilfrid**, built in 1950 but working anonymously until 1953.

Bord na Mona, the Irish Peat Commission, was established in 1946, taking over the bogs at Glenties (County Donegal) and Clonsast (County Offaly). Since then a large number of other areas have been acquired and Bord na Mona have laid down extensive railway systems on the 3 ft gauge for transporting the turf from the bogs to the various processing plants. While the great majority of the lines were operated by diesel traction, in County Offaly three turf-burning 0–6–0 well tank locomotives by Andrew Barclay Sons & Co Ltd were introduced in 1949, serving the ESB power station at Portarlington from the bogs of Clonsast and Garryhinch.

Shown here is the second of this trio, with a full load of turf waggons, at the Cushina level crossing in September 1950. The three steam locomotives have now been withdrawn.

Two standard 0–4–0T shunting locomotives of CSE (Comhlucht Siuicre Eireann) at Thurles in November 1951. These steam locomotives, now withdrawn, were built by Orenstein & Koppel of Berlin, three being supplied to each of the three beet-processing factories, at Thurles, Mallow and Tuam, in 1934-5.

TOURIST SERVICES AND BOAT TRAINS

From the last decade of the nineteenth century, Irish railway companies made a special effort to turn to their advantage the scenic attractions of those parts of the country served by their lines. As mobility of population increased with industrial prosperity in Great Britain, Ireland became a popular tourist area in which railway companies, both broad and narrow gauge, vied with each other to cater for the seasonal influx of visitors intent on admiring the scenic grandeur of Kerry or the unspoilt ruggedness of Connemara.

At Cobh, Rosslare, Dun Laoghaire, Greenore and Larne Harbour the railways ran right down to the quayside and provided direct access to the steamers. At Cobh (Queenstown) the American Mail tender moored alongside the station, while at Rosslare access to the boats was until very recently by rail only, there being no public road to the steamer berths. As Larne–Stranraer emerged as the official short sea route between Great Britain and the north of Ireland, so Larne Harbour grew in importance and covered station accommodation was provided, with trains running forward to the quayside under cover. At Greenore and Dun Laoghaire, too, the railway companies provided direct access from train to boat, and special trains were run in connection with steamer sailings from all these ports.

A somewhat different class of tourist traffic developed at that time in the immediate vicinity of the main towns and cities—excursion traffic catering for the day tripper from Dublin to Dun Laoghaire, Belfast to Bangor, Cork to Youghal, Londonderry to Buncrana. Here too the various railway companies did not fail to provide shuttle services in season, often at particularly attractive rates.

Tourist traffic in Ireland today is but a shadow of its former extent, mainly due to the massive increase in road transport, in both the public and private sectors. Both CIE and NIR operate special tourist facilities in season, on normal service workings, but gone are the days of the special tourist train, designed and made up to cater exclusively for a particular area and its company owned hotels. The flexibility of private road transport, and the ability thus afforded to many to tour areas hitherto reached only with some effort from peripheral rail-heads, has resulted in the emergence of holiday patterns very different from those of our grandparents.

Short haul tourist traffic has suffered even more severely and the lines from Dublin, Cork and Belfast formerly carrying thousands of day trippers in season are now kept open by the steady commuter traffic which they handle all year.

In 1903, in conjunction with Mr A. W. Holden, a Larne hotel proprietor, the Midland Railway (Northern Counties Committee) decided to build a new train for exclusive use on Holden's Popular Tour, which included 400 miles of rail travel, 40 miles of motor-coach drives and six days' hotel accommodation, all for £2 7s 6d. Three coaches in the train were bogie centre corridors, each seating forty-eight persons. The other coach in the train was a dining saloon, here running second, with a kitchen at one end. All these coaches had the lower panels finished in match boarding, with the crest and scroll lettering attached; the interior finishing was very grand with the upholstery in embossed gold leaf pattern. The tour train did not re-enter service after the Great War. The train is shown here at York Road in 1903 hauled by one of the new class of heavy compound engines designed by Mr Bowman Malcolm in 1901 and built in the Belfast shops of the BNCR. No 3, **King Edward VII**, was turned out in July 1902 and cost £2,843.

Shown here is the famous 'Tourist Train' of the Midland Great Western Railway, a through special which ran from Broadstone to Clifden once daily during the summer months, from 1903 to 1906. Stops were made at Mullingar, Athlone, Athenry, Galway and Oughterard and the train was equipped with a dining car. The train was painted in blue and white livery, the locomotive was blue, and this photograph, taken in 1905, shows **Arrow**, one of Martin Atock's standard 2–4–0 passenger engines of 1893, built at Broadstone in 1898, with the train at Clifden. A locomotive of this type was the last 2–4–0 in the world to work passenger traffic, on the Ballaghaderreen branch of the former MGWR in 1962.

In connection with the tourist traffic being promoted at the time, the Midland introduced ancillary road services from Westport and Clifden, connecting with the trains and traversing the wilds of Connemara, by Mweelrea, Killary Harbour and the Twelve Pins.

For many years Cobh (formerly Queenstown) has been the point of departure for tenders plying out to the trans-Atlantic liners anchored offshore. The Great Southern & Western Railway operated through mail services between Dublin and Cobh right up until the outbreak of World War I and these 'American Mails', as they were frequently called, incorporated a sorting carriage after the withdrawal of marine sorting offices on Cunard Packets in 1869. Here we see a local train at Queenstown in the 1890s headed by locomotive No 6 of the GS & WR, a 4 4 0 design by Alexander McDonnell built at Inchicore in 1877 and the first bogie engines in Ireland. The train is oil-lit.

The time interval separating these two views of boat trains on the Larne line is about forty years, yet each represents a distinctive phase in this particular branch of train working from York Road. The upper photograph, taken in 1896, shows a boat train in the new station at Larne Harbour. The locomotive is a 2–4–0 saddle tank, rebuilt by the Belfast & Northern Counties Railway Company at York Road in 1891 from Beyer Peacock's original side tank of 1883. The extent of the rail network in Antrim and Londonderry can be seen from the platform signboard.

The lower photograph, a fine action shot capturing much of the atmosphere of pre-war Northern Counties working, shows locomotive No 72, built originally in the Midland railway works at Derby in 1922 and rebuilt in 1937 at York Road, with the 'up' Stranraer boat express near Glynn, County Antrim, in August 1938.

The pier at Rosslare, County Wexford, was greatly extended early in the century with the construction of the line from Rosslare to Waterford, completed in 1906, and the introduction of regular steamer services from Rosslare to Fishguard in Pembrokeshire. This photograph is of particular interest in that it shows locomotive No 44, a small 4-4-0 whose regular job was on the pier at Rosslare but which on one memorable occasion acted as pilot for the main line working to Waterford. The railways at Rosslare are in two parts, the line to the pier, and the mainland section with engine shed and turntable at Ballygeary. Until 1964 motorists wishing to ship their cars from Rosslare had to have them brought out to the ferry by train as there was no road access.

Despite being $26\tfrac{3}{4}$ miles distant, Youghal has long been the traditional excursion outlet for Cork city. Though some distance from the town centre, the station is well situated for the thousands of day trippers who over the years have come to the resort. This photograph, taken some sixty years ago, reminds one of the unrivalled position then enjoyed by the railways in handling heavy excursion traffic between fixed terminals; indeed, this is one section of passenger traffic for which the railways have always been ideally suited and for which they still continue to cater, though on a greatly reduced scale.

On the Great Southern & Western the most famous tourist train was probably the 'Killarney Express', introduced in 1898, which took 4 hours, with four or five stops, to cover the 185 miles from Kingsbridge. The 'Killarney Express' ceased running with the outbreak of hostilities in August 1914. Shown here leaving Kingsbridge, the express is hauled by locomotive No 321, a 4–4–0 main line passenger express engine built at Inchicore in 1904.

(Opposite) Killarney was the terminus of the line from Mallow from when it opened in July 1853 until the rail head was driven on to Tralee in 1859. As the fame of the area as a tourist mecca began to spread, the GS & WR built a large hotel immediately adjoining the railway station. From there a wide range of tours throughout the surrounding country was introduced and here we see an open car about to leave the hotel for a tour of the lakes, sometime around 1905.

Opened in June 1901, the Hill of Howth Tramway—a 5 ft 3 in gauge railway worked by electric tramcars—was built by the Great Northern Railway (Ireland) to open up the residential area recently developed there and to provide access to the Hill for seasonal tourist traffic. The line closed in May 1959. Access to the 'tramway' was from Sutton station on the Howth branch of the Great Northern line from Dublin to the north, and from here round the head to Howth was a distance of $5\frac{1}{4}$ miles. Our illustration shows Tramcars Nos 7, 4, 1 and 10 at Sutton in the early days, around 1910.

In the north the Belfast & County Down Railway Company hit upon the novel idea of operating pleasure paddle steamers between Belfast, Larne, Portrush and some of the smaller ports of the Ards peninsula. Tickets were issued at Belfast both for round trips by sea to Bangor and Larne and also for round trips to these same places involving an outward journey by sea and a return journey by rail. Seen here at Bangor's North Pier is **Erin's Isle**, a paddle steamer built for the railway company in 1912 and in service until the autumn of 1915.

The boat trains on the Ballymena & Larne Railway were the fastest narrow-gauge workings in Ireland. Under the Midland Railway (Northern Counties Committee) the Ballymena & Larne Railway introduced an express boat train which completed the 25¼ mile run from Ballymena to Larne Harbour in exactly one hour. Here the Larne boat train leaves Ballymena in the early 1930s hauled by ex-Ballycastle Railway 4–4–2T No 113 built by Kitson & Co of Leeds in 1908. The leading carriage (No 350) is a composite first and third class coach, with central corridor, end vestibules, lavatory accommodation and electric light. All three carriages here, Nos 350, 352 and 353, were built by the LMS (NCC) at York Road in 1928 and were by far the most advanced narrow-gauge stock ever to run in Ireland.

The coastal scenery traversed by the Belfast–Coleraine–Londonderry line of the LMS (NCC) was of outstanding natural beauty. The great basalt cliffs between Castlerock and Downhill had posed a formidable problem for the early railway engineers working on the Londonderry & Coleraine Railway. Two tunnels, one 700 yd, the other 300 yd in length, were cut through the cliffs, partly by pick and shovel and partly by a major explosion on Saturday 6 June 1846, by which 30,000 tons of rock were loosened at the western end of the shorter, more westerly tunnel. A contemporary report, describing the scene, considered the blast as 'second only in importance to the great explosion of the chalk cliffs at the Shakespeare Tunnel on the Dover railway...'

Here the Derry train, headed by locomotive No 61, **County Antrim**, of the LMS (NCC) emerges from the western mouth of the short tunnel, below the Mussenden Temple, on 18 June 1938. This was precisely the area cleared by blasting in 1846.

Belfast and Northern Counties Railway.
Glenariff, Cushendall & Garron Tower.

Scale of Charges for the conveyance of Passengers to and from Parkmore Station.

The following **CAR OWNERS** have agreed not to exceed the undernoted scale of charges:—

Henry McNeill, Ltd.	Charles Relly	John Reid
Charles McAllister	Patrick Kelly	John Murphy
Hugh Mullan	John McDade	Robert Sharp
Patrick Reilly	Charles McLoughlin	Wm. J. McFettridge
John McAuley	John Boyd	Jas. McAuley
Hugh Boyd	J. McWilliams	Wm. Murchrell
Thomas Reid	Patrick Kerr	

	Each Passenger	Minimum Charge
I. Between Parkmore Station and entrance of Glen	3d	6d
II. From Parkmore Station to entrance of Glen, and from Glenfoot to Cushendall (allowing 1½ hours in the Glen)	1/-	4/-
III. From Parkmore Station to entrance of Glen, and from Glenfoot to Cushendall and back to Parkmore same day	1/6	6/-
IV. Tea House to Parkmore Station	9d	2/-
V. From Parkmore Station to entrance of Glen and back from Glenfoot same day	1/-	4/-
VI. From Parkmore Station to Garron Tower (via the Glen) and back to Parkmore direct same day	2/-	8/-
Ditto (if back by way of Cushendall)	2/6	9/-
VII. Public Car leaves Parkmore daily at 10-45 a.m. for Garron Tower, returning at 3-30, p.m. Return Fare	2/-	
VIII. From Parkmore to Cushendun, via Vale of Glenariff and Cushendall, and back to Parkmore same day	2/6	8/-
IX. Special Car or other vehicle with Refreshments, etc., Parkmore Station to Tea House, inclusive of whip money	2/3 per vehicle	
X. Ditto, with unconsumed Refreshments, Empties, etc., Tea House to Parkmore Station	2/6	,,
XI. Ditto for double journey if employed at time of commencing outward journey	4/-	,,
XII. Small packages (Baskets, etc.), from Parkmore Station to Tea House, belonging to parties who use Car as far as Parkmore Post Office and walk through the Glen — Up to 14 lbs. **2d** each. Up to 28 lbs. **3d** ,,		Minimum charge 2/3 per vehicle.
XIII. Ditto, for parties who do not use Car as far as Post Office — Up to 14 lbs. **4d** ,, Up to 28 lbs. **6d** ,,		

Passengers are warned not to listen to any proposals regarding conveyances at Parkmore that may be made to them, by persons in the Train, and are respectfully requested to call the attention of the Guard to any case of annoyance caused by such persons.

To avoid excessive demands visitors should only engage Cars bearing the names of the Owners enumerated above, or otherwise make a bargain before engagement.

Belfast—M'Crea & M'Farland, Ltd., Agents.

A publicity brochure of c 1900 speaks eloquently of the various tourist facilities available to travellers on the Parkmore line of the Belfast & Northern Counties system.

Nor was the BNCR restricted to organising rail and road transport for its patrons. In the Islandmagee peninsula, in the south-east corner of County Antrim, the great basalt cliffs at 'The Gobbins' provide a coastline of great natural beauty. To encourage rail traffic from Belfast and Larne to Whitehead, the nearest station, the Northern Counties erected a series of footpaths around the cliffs, with spectacular bridges of various designs linking the several sections high above the sea.

For many years the north Down resort of Bangor benefited from a great seasonal influx of excursion traffic passing from the Great Northern system over the metals of the former Belfast Central Railway on to the Belfast & County Down Railway on the other side of the Lagan at a junction lying just outside the Queen's Quay terminus. From Lisburn, Lurgan, Portadown and frequently from much further afield excursion specials brought Sunday School children, Orangemen, Women's Institutes, Young Farmers, football supporters, bandsmen and countless other less clearly defined parties of one sort or another.

With the reorganisation of much of central Belfast's traffic flow and the construction of a new road bridge over the Lagan, through running as described has been impossible since 1965, though under a new ten-year programme of development, recently announced by the Northern Ireland Government, it seems probable that the line will be reopened.

Shown here is a return Bangor–Dublin excursion train crossing the Lagan Bridge on 22 July 1937, headed by GNR (I) 0–6–0, No 78.

COMMUTER SERVICES AND LOCAL TRAINS

Around Dublin, Cork and Belfast the growth of suburbia and the development of residential, dormitory towns and suburbs lying within daily travelling distance of the city centre led to the emergence of a wide range of local train services in these areas, catering for this commuter traffic. Some of the services were operated by unusual and noteworthy rail vehicles and a few of these are considered in greater detail in a later section. Here we are concerned more with the character of the lines and the nature of the traffic.

The short line from Harcourt Road to Bray was opened by the Dublin & Wicklow Railway Company on 10 July 1854 but Harcourt Street Station in Dublin was not opened until 7 February 1859. The line closed down at the end of 1958. As the city spread southwards, towards the foothills of the Wicklow mountains, a heavy business traffic developed on the Harcourt Street line, from Shankill, Carrickmines, Foxrock, Stillorgan and Dundrum. Here locomotive No 198, a 'J15' built at Inchicore in 1899 but with a 'Z'-type boiler of 1933, passes through Carrickmines in 1955 with a Harcourt Street–Bray train.

The other line to Bray, that of the original Dublin & Kingstown Railway as it was extended by Dalkey and Killiney, adhered closely to the shore and severe flooding of the track during heavy seas and periods of onshore gales often caused disruption of services. This view of Blackrock station in March 1937 stresses the point and emphasises the value of having at that time an alternative line of rail communication to Bray, Wicklow and Rosslare.

One of the earliest suburban railways in Ireland was the Belfast Central Railway, completed in 1875 and linking the Great Northern and County Down systems across the Lagan. Attempts to cater for short distance passenger traffic in south Belfast, with stations at Donegall Road, Botanic Road, Ormeau and the Queen's Bridge, were thwarted by the simultaneous emergence of the Belfast horse tramway system, and passenger services were withdrawn as early as 1885. Shown here is a local train at Ulster Junction around 1880.

'101' class locomotive No 126, built at Inchicore in 1881, with an 'up' local train of six-wheelers, passing Tivoli station on the Cork–Youghal line just outside Cork in the early 1920s. The station here was closed in 1931. Apart from Dublin and Belfast, Cork was the only centre with special commuter services.

The short Bangor line out of Belfast, along the south shore of Belfast Lough, has always been one of the main commuter lines in the country and here a general platform view about the turn of the century, with the arrival of the Bangor train at Queen's Quay, reflects the importance of this branch of passenger traffic at that time.

This Bangor line, with its heavy surburban commuter traffic, was the scene of a serious accident towards the end of World War II, as workers for the large shipyard and aircraft factory poured in from the surrounding countryside. In the early morning darkness of 10 January 1945, between Victoria Park Halt and Ballymacarrett Junction, twenty-three persons were killed and forty-one injured in an accident which did much to hasten the eclipse of the independent Belfast & County Down Railway Company and indirectly contributed much towards the withdrawal of rail services from the greater part of the county.

A push and pull 'motor train' from Holywood ran into the back of a stationary workmen's train consisting of thirteen six-wheelers. The heavy leading bogie coach of the motor train, driven forward by the steam locomotive in the rear, ploughed into the rake of passenger coaches, mounted the underframe of the end coach and telescoped forward on to the chassis of the next coach in line. All the dead were in the last two carriages of the workmen's train.

Here the break-down crane lifts the motor train driving bogie from the underframe of the carriage demolished on impact.

A local train (Belfast–Portadown) leaves Great Victoria Street in July 1945, hauled by a GN 4–4–2T (class 'T2'), No 139, built by Nasmyth Wilson in 1924, a class of locomotive which did much valuable work on suburban traffic around Belfast and Dublin over a forty-year period. The train itself is of some interest too, in that the rake of coaches comprises mixed GN and (ex) GS & WR stock, running in the north as a result of the wartime emergency.

From the early years of this century there occurred a remarkable increase in the short-haul passenger traffic moving up and down the Lagan valley, particularly between Belfast and Lisburn. Rail motors were introduced to handle this expanding commuter traffic but they proved unable to cope with the numbers travelling and orthodox 'push and pull' trains took over. By the early 1930s Lisburn was being served by no less than fifty-four weekday trains in each direction, a figure which rose to over seventy during World War II.

Shown here is an 'up' local 'motor train' at Adelaide in August 1932. The train is being propelled from the rear by a conventional steam locomotive controlled by the driver from a cab up front and with the fireman on the footplate fixing the position of the reversing lever as instructed by telegraph. This was an adaptation of the original Great Northern 'push and pull' trains of earlier in the century, where the steam locomotive was sandwiched between two special driving coaches. The white square, hung on the smoke box door, was an indication that the locomotive here was driving in reverse. The engine is No 30, a 4-4-2T belonging to a class built for the GNR by Beyer Peacock and Nasmyth Wilson between 1921 and 1930 and much used on local trains in the Belfast and Dublin areas.

RAILWAY ARCHITECTURE AND DESIGN AFTER 1870

The last quarter of the nineteenth century, and the opening years of the twentieth, witnessed the emergence of certain distinctive styles in Irish railway architecture resulting from amalgamation and subsequent standardisation on several of the principal systems, the construction of branch lines into areas of low potential return, the emergence of an extensive and significant narrow-gauge network and, finally, the introduction of new building materials, and with these, of revolutionary techniques in railway engineering.

The design of station buildings by the main companies was now more a matter for the civil engineer than the architect. Blueprint designs emerged which were applied again and again on stations being built after 1870, interrupted here and there perhaps by designs resulting from the existence of special circumstances or the personal insistence of influential citizens. On branch lines, often constructed tongue in cheek with a minimum of expenditure, it was unlikely that much money would be sunk into ornate designs or individually styled railway buildings. Thus, buildings at branch line stations created after 1870 are in the main plain and functional, with a minimum of flourish in design or execution. The same could be said of the architecture and design of the great majority of narrow-gauge stations, though occasionally the buoyant optimism of the early days of these light railways is reflected in more extravagant expressions.

The introduction of new building materials and of new techniques of construction affected line structures of civil engineering more than station buildings. It is reflected in the pre-cast and reinforced concrete sheds, bridges and viaducts of the Midland Railway and of the London Midland & Scottish Railway (Northern Counties Committee) in Ulster; the steel girder bridges on the Rosslare–Waterford line in south Leinster or on the Achill and Clifden branches of the Midland Great Western in Connaught; and in the incorporation of combinations of brick, concrete, steel sheet or girder and traditional stone masonry in many of the railway bridges and viaducts built after 1880 eg, on the Keady branch of the Great Northern, the Valentia branch of the Great Southern & Western or the narrow-gauge lines in County Donegal.

In 1877 W. H. Mills became the first chief civil engineer of the GNR (I) and the great majority of the stations built on the Great Northern in the years which followed were to his design. In polychrome brick, often yellow with relieving courses in brown, red and black, Mills' design was flexible and could be adapted to a wide range of buildings. A good example of a large station built to his design was Dundalk, completed in 1893.

The station at Sion Mills, County Tyrone, is an excellent example of Mills' design as applied to a small country station, with buildings on the 'down' platform only and incorporating living accommodation for stationmaster and family in the main block. The station here dates from 1883 and this general view of the station buildings, from the north east, was taken about 1905.

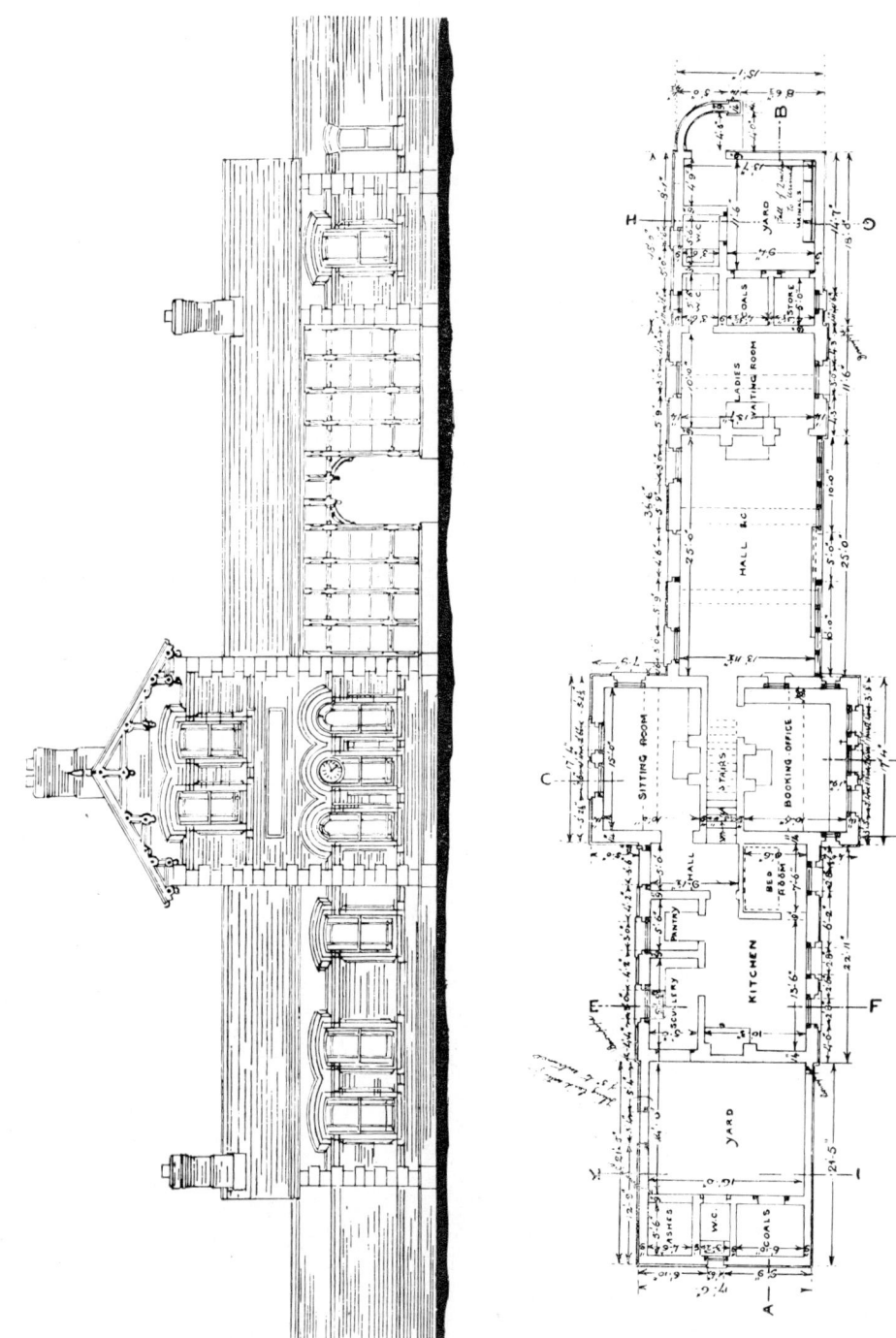

The original architectural drawings for many Great Northern stations of this period have survived and here we see (top) a platform elevation of the main station building at Sion Mills with, below, a ground plan of same.

The station at Portrush is in the 'Swiss chalet' style of the Belfast & Northern Counties Railway Company and is a remarkable exercise in black and white timber sheeting 'Mock Tudor', over a red brick shell. It dates from 1893.

This platform view at Queenstown (Cobh), taken perhaps sixty to seventy years ago, illustrates graceful yet functional cast-iron columns and brackets which supported light transverse girders carrying the main platform canopy of timber and glass. Much of the cast-iron work on Irish railway station platforms was of local design and manufacture though in the north there is a great deal from Scottish foundries. Note here the pendant gas lanterns and the unusual passenger carriages, extreme right.

The Waterside terminus of the Belfast & Northern Counties Railway in Londonderry, completed in 1887, is an attractive building in dressed granite, with living accommodation and an Italianate clock tower reminiscent of Connolly Station in Dublin.

The interior of the Belfast terminus of the Northern Counties system, at York Road, seen here at the turn of the century, displays an ornate style in wood-carving, with high-pitched roofs, clock towers, rustic seating and lavish timber panelling characteristic of the continental influence permeating much of the Belfast company's ideas on design at this time.

With many of the early wooden bridges, thirty years of regular use resulted in such depreciation that by the last quarter of the century many had to be replaced by new girder structures, sometimes resting on existing masonry piers, elsewhere part of entirely new constructions. The bridge at Thomastown, County Kilkenny, for example, '... a stupendous work' on the Waterford & Kilkenny Railway, spanning the river Nore and completed in 1850, had to be completely replaced as early as 1876.

The viaduct at Killyhevlin (Weir's Bridge) on the Sligo Leitrim & Northern Counties Railway near Enniskillen, built in 1877-8, illustrates the changing character of viaduct construction from the early days, with a much greater proportion of the total structure, including the central piers, consisting of ironwork.

Two street views of the period in Dublin and Belfast are of interest in a general railway context. The Amiens Street terminus of the GNR (I) decorated for the Irish visit of George V in the summer of 1911 with, below, a famous landmark in east Belfast, now demolished—the 'Holywood Arches'—by which the main line of the BCDR system was carried across two busy suburban roads. The complete absence of mechanically driven road vehicles and the electric tramway service suggest a date around 1910.

One aspect of railway working hitherto not represented but one without which no railway could function was that of signalling. Here we see (top) a typical signal cabin interior, at Ballymacarrett Junction on the Belfast & County Down Railway, just outside the Queen's Quay terminus, as recorded in the early years of this century, with (below) gantries of semaphore signals at Queen's Quay, operated by manual leverage and now replaced by electrically controlled colour signals.

The three viaducts here, all dating from between 1890 and 1910, reflect the predominance of the girder lattice framework at this time, in striking contrast to the great stone viaducts of the early days of railway construction, at Bessbrook, Mallow and Randalstown.

Above, the Corrib viaduct at Galway on the Midland Great Western branch line to Clifden, 1893; below, a view of the Suir viaduct on the Waterford–Rosslare line under construction in 1903-4; opposite, the narrow-gauge viaduct of the Strabane & Letterkenny Railway across the Foyle at Lifford, 1907.

Two short tunnels constructed within a year or so of each other in the early 1890s, at Drung Hill, County Kerry (top) and Newport, County Mayo, reflect the sustained perseverance of the railway engineers in the closing years of the nineteenth century in extending rail-heads out to the western seaboard, far from major centres of population and through areas from which there was little potential return, save in a certain amount of seasonal tourist traffic.

A viaduct constructed in the early years of this century, at Tassagh, near Keady, in County Armagh, on the Castleblayney Keady & Armagh Railway (1903-1910) reflects clearly the use of new building materials in combination—concrete piers, with brick facings on each of the eleven arches, and brick courses on the underside of each span. Altogether a lighter structure than the early masonry viaducts and one in which stone, brick and concrete blended quite successfully, though with less durability.

LOCOMOTIVE DEVELOPMENT AFTER 1900

Irish locomotive development in the present century began with a sudden and substantial increase in the size of engines due largely to the introduction of bogie stock, dining cars and, in general, of much heavier trains. There was a secondary watershed around 1913-16 with the introduction of superheating but thereafter, while the size of locomotives increased, the introduction of new types became rare. The last steam locomotives built in Ireland—apart from Bulleid's turf burner—were constructed at Inchicore on the eve of World War II, and the last conventional steam locomotives introduced on Irish railways entered service on the Sligo Leitrim & Northern Counties line in the summer of 1951.

MGWR locomotive No 124, **Mercuric**, a 4-4-0 passenger express engine built at Broadstone in 1905 to a design by Edward Cusack, chief mechanical engineer from 1901 to 1915. As photographed here, outside the Broadstone shops, the locomotive is as rebuilt by Cusack's successor, W. H. Morton, in 1916, though even in its original form Morton's ideas were clearly evident. The engine subsequently became CIE No 550 and was withdrawn from service in 1957.

On the London Midland & Scottish Railway (Northern Counties Committee) the success of the five 4-4-0 passenger locomotives built for the company by the North British Locomotive Company in 1924 (class 'U2') prompted the Board to order five more of these engines towards the end of that year, three to be built at York Road in Belfast and two by the North British. No 80 (opposite, above) heading an 'up' Larne branch line train at Whiteabbey in August 1953, was completed at York Road in November 1925 and named **Dunseverick Castle** in 1933. Based on Bowman Malcolm's 'U' class of 1914, but fitted with Midland Class 2 boiler, cab and tender, these engines proved very successful and No 80 was not withdrawn from service until 1961. A locomotive of this class, No 74, **Dunluce Castle**, is preserved in the Ulster Transport Museum.

In 1920 Beyer Peacock built four large 4-6-4 tanks, Nos 22-25, for the Belfast & County Down Railway Company. These engines, each weighing over 81 tons, were the heaviest tank locomotives on any Irish line until the arrival of the first of the 'Jeeps' on the LMS (NCC) in 1946. Owing to their weight these massive 'Baltic' tanks were kept on the Bangor branch and they became a characteristic feature of that line until 1956. Here No 24 heads a 'down' Bangor train of mixed six-wheelers and bogie stock at Queen's Quay on 19 June 1948. The rake of coaches is passing beneath what was the largest signal gantry in Ireland.

In April 1911 an interesting interchange of locomotives occurred on Irish railways, involving engines representative of main line passenger express locomotive development at that time on two of the principal railway companies, the Great Northern and the Great Southern & Western.

Neptune, No 113 on the GN, a 'QL' class 4–4–0 built to Charles Clifford's design by the North British Locomotive Co, Glasgow in 1904, to handle the increasing weight of passenger trains on main line workings, was exchanged for a week with GS & WR locomotive No 322, a 4–4–0 with characteristic cone-shaped boiler, built at Inchicore in the same year to a design by Robert Coey. '113' ran from Dublin to Cork, '322' from Dublin to Belfast, and the main finding of the interchange was that the northern engine proved superior in coal consumption but that the Inchicore engine was superior in various fittings, particularly in lubrication.

The reasons behind the interchange, initiative for which came from the Great Northern, may have been to compare a 'QL' with a contemporary southern engine in view of the fact that Clifford's design was by then over six years old and locomotives of this class were being fully extended on main line workings. At any rate, shortly after the trials the most famous of all Clifford's locomotive types, the 4–4–0 'S' class—with a corresponding class of goods engine—made their appearance on the Great Northern system.

The photograph of '322' reproduced here (opposite) was taken at Belfast during the locomotive interchange of 1911.

Two locomotives of the Londonderry & Lough Swilly Railway Company deserve inclusion here. Firstly, a 4–8–0 tender locomotive (above), No 12, built by Hudswell Clarke of Leeds to a design by James Conner, locomotive superintendent, which was one of two such engines introduced in 1905 to work the long Burtonport extension of the Swilly system without taking coal. They were the first engines in Ireland with eight-coupled wheels and the only tender engines ever to run on the Irish narrow gauge. No 12 continued in use on the Burtonport line until the closure in June 1947.

In 1912 Hudswell Clarke built the last engines for the Swilly railway company, two massive 4–8–4 tank locomotives, each weighing nearly 59 tons in full working order, the largest ever to run on the Irish narrow gauge. These engines, Nos 5 and 6 in the Swilly stock, continued in use until the system closed down and were cut up for scrap in 1954.

One of the most outstanding of all Irish locomotive classes was the 'S' class of the Great Northern, a batch of five 4–4–0 passenger express locomotives built for the company by Beyer Peacock in 1912-13. Numbered 170-174, each was originally named after a famous Irish mountain. The design was by Charles Clifford, who retired in May 1912, nine months before the engines were delivered. No 174, **Carrantuohill**, worked the first non-stop train from Belfast to Dublin on 26 February 1914 (112.6 miles in 116 minutes), though with a light load. During the first three years of the Great War the 'S' class engines had so much in hand that the GNR (I) was able to continue improving its services while those of almost all other companies were deteriorating. The 'Limited Mails' between Dublin and Belfast regularly took only $2\frac{1}{2}$ hours, including three stops totalling 10 minutes, and even after the introduction of the large three-cylinder compounds in the early 1930s the 'S' class, by now operating with increased boiler pressure of 200 psi, put in some of the finest running ever accomplished on Irish railways.

As delivered, the engines were green, with black and red detail, and each was individually named. Soon after Glover's arrival they were painted black and the names were removed around 1920. They were repainted blue, and renamed as before, during a complete rebuilding at Dundalk in 1938-9. No 171, **Slieve Gullion**, has been preserved by the Railway Preservation Society of Ireland and has recently undergone major repairs in Harland & Wolff's Belfast shops.

Seen here at Great Victoria Street, Belfast, on the 2.45 pm Dublin train on 1 August 1932, is No 174, black and nameless yet somehow a design epitomising all the elegant power of the steam locomotive at its best.

A small class of 4–6–0 mixed traffic engines designed by J. R. Bazin and built at Inchicore between 1924 and 1926, the three 500s (class 'B1') had 5 ft 8½ in driving wheels and two outside cylinders measuring 19½ in × 28 in. Though built as mixed traffic engines they were used almost entirely for main line passenger work. Their relatively small coupled wheels allowed lively acceleration and good uphill work and the engines had a top speed of around 75 mph. No 502, built at Inchicore in 1926 and withdrawn in 1957, is seen here on the main line at Portarlington in the summer of 1947.

A 2–4–2 compound narrow-gauge tank engine built at York Road in 1909, one of six built between 1892 and 1920 to a design by Bowman Malcolm, locomotive superintendent to the Belfast & Northern Counties Railway Company, and its successors. Of the six engines built, the first two were by Beyer Peacock, the last four by the York Road shops. No 101 (built as No 113), seen here at Ballymoney in August 1933, had a coal bunker fitted to the rear of the cab in July 1928, lengthening the engine and wheelbase by 2 ft. It was renumbered again in June 1939 and as '41' ran on the Ballycastle line until the closure in July 1950.

In 1932 work on the renewal of the Boyne viaduct at Drogheda was completed and, in keeping with a general acceleration of railway schedules, the Great Northern introduced new timetables which marked the zenith of the company's achievement in passenger train working. To deal with these schedules a batch of five three-cylinder compound locomotives was built by Beyer Peacock to G. T. Glover's design. Numbered 83-7 and named **Eagle**, **Falcon**, **Merlin**, **Peregrine** and **Kestrel**, the axle load of these new engines was 21 tons, the maximum allowance, and their original working boiler pressure was 250 psi, subsequently reduced to 200 psi when the very fast schedules of 1932 and 1933 were eased out in the following year.

The compounds coped smoothly with the demanding timetables, and speeds of over 80 mph in normal service were commonplace. The main line trains, between Dublin and Belfast, ran five times each way daily and were allowed an average overall time of 2 hours and 28 minutes, including Customs examination and all stops, but the *average running time* was 2 hours $9\frac{3}{4}$ minutes, as compared with the 2 hours 15 minutes allowed for the non-stop 'Enterprise Express', introduced in 1947.

Seen here shortly after coming into service, in Glover's black livery, on the 5.30 pm 'up' Mail at Great Victoria Street, Belfast, on 1 June 1932, is No 85, **Merlin**, a locomotive now in store for the Ulster Transport Museum.

In the autumn of 1946 the LMS (NCC) introduced the first four of a batch of eighteen 2–6–4 tank locomotives (class 'WT') which were considered suitable for working the compact Northern Counties system. Apart from the two locomotives by Beyer Peacock introduced on the SL & NCR in 1951, the last eight engines in this 'WT' class, built at Derby in 1949-50, were the last steam locomotives constructed for Irish railways. They were built in such a way as to be similar (with interchangeable parts) to the 2–6–0 mixed traffic 'Moguls'. Driving wheels were 6 ft in diameter, cylinders 19 in × 26 in, boiler pressure 200 psi and full working weight 87 tons. The nickname 'Jeep' was given to the first batch by a foreman impressed by their general handiness and all-purpose design, and has stayed with them ever since. In recent years their main duty has been in hauling the 'spoil' trains from Magheramorne to Belfast (see page 99), and at the time of writing the last few survivors in the class are the only steam locomotives still in occasional main line service in the British Isles.

Here, No 5, the first of the class, prepares to leave Larne Harbour with the 6 pm 'up' working on 24 April 1948.

SPECIAL SERVICES AND ROYAL TRAINS

In addition to the regular tourist facilities provided by the principal railway companies, a large number of the special trains run on Irish railways at one time or another were prompted by occasions as diverse as royal visits, troop and livestock movements, security patrols, rugby internationals, GAA matches, religious pilgrimages and numerous demonstrations and celebrations of sectarian origin. On these occasions, with the exception of visits by royalty when special trains were provided superbly fitted out in the style of the period, it was not uncommon to see long rakes of carriages, heterogeneous in composition and often including old rolling stock normally kept in the seclusion of some quiet corner of the carriage shops, pressed into service to cope with the abnormal volume of traffic existing on that particular day. It was on these specials, too, that of late years the railway enthusiast had his best chance of seeing steam locomotives in action. Even before the eclipse of steam on normal working throughout the country, the types and combinations of locomotives in service with these special trains, often out of their normal context, was a source of great interest and delight to the steam enthusiast.

The interior of the Royal Saloon on the Belfast & County Down Railway Company's Royal Train of July 1903, used on the occasion of a visit by King Edward VII and Queen Alexandra, is a perfect reflection of Edwardian taste run riot and a fine example of Irish Royal Saloons of the period.

An Orange demonstration special at Donegal town on 12 July 1906. On occasions like this all available rolling stock was pressed into service.

A 'down' livestock 'Fair Special' of empty waggons at Hill of Down in February 1955 on the main MGWR line to Mullingar and Athlone. The fattening lands of Kildare, Meath, Westmeath, Laois, Offaly and Roscommon provided the Midland with an important traffic for many years, long trains of lime-washed waggons being run out from Dublin in connection with the great livestock fairs. The engine is a mixed traffic 0–6–0 built at Broadstone in 1924.

Between the wars the Belfast & County Down Railway ran special services each year in connection with the famous international Tourist Trophy Motor Car Race, run over the Ards Circuit, on public roads between Dundonald, Comber and Newtownards. Here locomotive No 10, an 0–6–0 goods engine built by Beyer Peacock in 1914, is seen in a role in which both Nos 10 and 4 (a second 0–6–0 goods locomotive from the same maker, delivered in 1921) were often cast, hauling heavy excursion trains or, as here, special workings on both main and branch lines. This particular view is of No 10 leaving Comber for Belfast on the evening of 7 September 1935, after the race, with a long rake of characteristic 'County Down' six-wheelers.

During the inter-war years, to cater for that large section of the public for whom the motor car was as yet an expensive luxury, the Great Southern Railways Company, formed by amalgamation in 1925, ran a wide range of special trains from Dublin. Particularly popular were the mystery tours, which continue to operate today, and here a Mystery Train at Cashel in May 1939 is hauled by locomotive No 342, one of five 4–4–0s built at Inchicore in 1936 as an improved addition to the 'D4' class of 1907-8.

The Civil War of 1922-3 resulted in the regular patrolling of the railways by the army, with frequent battles between the Irish Free State Army Railway Repair and Maintenance Corps and the anti-treaty forces. The two photographs included here reflect the emergency: above, two armoured rail-cars of the corps at Cork in November 1922 with, opposite, locomotive No 102 of the MGWR at Mullingar early in 1923 with a railway maintenance corps patrol. An innocuous 0–6–0 shunting tank, **Pilot**, built at Broadstone in 1881, this engine shed its armour plating in August 1923 and returned to normal duties soon afterwards. The temporary inscription reflects one of the main international news stories of the time.

On Sunday 26 June 1949, the Pioneer Total Abstinence Association Jubilee in Dublin, together with major GAA matches in Kilkenny and Limerick, resulted in the heaviest passenger traffic in Ireland since the Eucharistic Congress of 1932. Thirty-one special trains converged on Dublin and here the 'up' special from Killeshandra and Edenderry on the Midland section leaves Leixlip, double-headed by CIE locomotives Nos 594 and 657, both ex-MGWR engines **Inny** and **Arrow** respectively.

The 'Bundoran Express', one of Ireland's relatively few named trains, was introduced during World War II; a daily summer train from Dublin to Bundoran aimed primarily at the heavy seasonal pilgrimage traffic to Lough Derg in County Donegal, for which Pettigo was the nearest station. The 'down' service stopped at Drogheda, Dundalk and Clones and ran thence to Pettigo without stopping at either Enniskillen or Bundoran Junction, thus obviating the necessity for Customs examination. Belfast passengers for Pettigo and Bundoran could join the train at Clones. This view of the 'up' working at Pettigo was taken shortly before rail services were withdrawn from west Ulster in the autumn of 1957 and shows the 'down' and 'up' expresses crossing, with the latter headed by No 204, **Antrim**, one of a batch of five 4–4–0s built by Beyer Peacock in 1948.

The Cork Industrial Fair and Exhibition lasted from May to October 1932. A miniature railway was laid down in the grounds at Carrigrohane Road and two locomotives, semi-scale 4-6-2 tender engines inscribed 'Brangschbahnen–Leipzig' were brought over from Germany, along with a set of open-sided coaches. The miniature railway proved one of the highlights of the exhibition and both locomotives and rolling stock were returned to Germany at the end of the season.

In July 1937 King George VI and Queen Elizabeth visited Belfast and were greeted by thousands of the province's youth at the Showgrounds, Balmoral. Numerous additional trains were run in connection with the event and here at Balmoral, on the evening of 28 July, we see a Great Northern special bound for Belleek in the extreme west of the province, headed by No 171, **Slieve Gullion**, one of the memorable 'S' class of the GNR(I) to which attention has already been drawn. This locomotive is preserved in running order by the Railway Preservation Society of Ireland.

From 1936 heavy seasonal pilgrimage traffic has existed to Claremorris, County Mayo, for the village of Knock, ten miles to the north, where supernatural visions of a highly spiritual character had been reported as early as 1879. The Marian Year (1954) saw an exceptional volume of pilgrimage traffic moving to and from Claremorris all through the summer, and here a special train at Claremorris on 27 June of that year is headed by a 2–6–0 Woolwich engine of the Midland Great Western, one of twelve such locomotives assembled at the Broadstone shops between 1925 and 1927 from sets of parts made at the Woolwich Arsenal in the immediate post-war years. In addition, this is a Radio Train, a service introduced by CIE in 1949 on the centenary run from Dublin to Cork, with facilities for the transmission of suitable material over an internal radio system from a mobile studio.

(Opposite) The Royal Train of 3 July 1953, as used for the journey from Lisburn to Lisahally during the visit of Queen Elizabeth II and the Duke of Edinburgh. The locomotive here is No 102 from the former LMS (NCC) fleet, a 2–6–0 mixed traffic engine—a class 'W' Mogul—assembled at York Road from parts brought over from Derby and completed in April 1940. Fifteen of these engines were brought into service on the LMS system between 1933 and 1942, the earlier ones built in Derby, the later engines assembled in Belfast, and the last survivor of the class, No 97, the **Earl of Ulster**, was scrapped in 1965. The train here consists of combined GN and UTA stock, all painted in Great Northern blue and cream livery.

STEAM CARRIAGES, INSPECTION VEHICLES, RAIL-CARS AND BUSES, ROLLING STOCK

The former existence of a large number of relatively small systems, fused together by progressive amalgamations into the great national networks of the peak years of Irish railway working, resulted in the survival into quite recent times of a number of interesting rail vehicles, as diverse in origin as they were singular in appearance. These included steam carriages on the GS & WR, the GNR (I), the BCDR and the BNCR, the push-pull trains of the Great Northern—successors to the steam carriages on short distance commuter traffic, both north and south—various inspection cars and trolleys, the revolutionary track layer designed by A. W. Bretland of the Midland and introduced, after amalgamation, on the Great Southern Railways early in 1925, and a number of interesting and significant coaches and carriages from both broad and narrow gauge.

While some of these have found their way to the Transport Museum in Belfast, or have survived by some other means, the majority had already disappeared before the public conscience was sufficiently aware of the importance of keeping such railway curiosities for the enlightenment and mystification of future generations.

This 0–4–2T steam carriage, **Fairy**, was built at Inchicore in 1894 with the carriage portion mounted on a separate four-wheel frame permanently close-coupled to the engine. Designed originally as an inspection vehicle, an earlier steam carriage, **Sprite**, had been rebuilt as a pay carriage in 1873 and it was for this purpose that **Fairy** was designed by Alexander McDonnell in 1894. The entrance to the mobile pay carriage was from a covered platform at the back, having steps each side, so that the men being paid could go up, collect their money at a hatch and go down the far side. Abolition of the pay carriage system in 1926 resulted in the withdrawal of both **Sprite** and **Fairy**.

Two steam motor carriages were ordered by the Midland Railway (NCC) from Derby in 1905. These had already become quite fashionable in Britain for use on branch line services and it was natural that their use should spread to Ireland on a system controlled by a subsidiary of the Midland. They were really a bogie coach of standard design except that instead of the conventional bogie the steel underframe was pivoted at one end to a small 0–2–2 side tank locomotive. This had two outside cylinders located under the cab, driving forward to the front pair of wheels, each 3 ft $7\frac{1}{2}$ in in diameter. Seating capacity of the coach was six first class, sixteen second class and twenty-four third class. The coaches were fitted with a driving compartment at the rear end so that the driver could change over when travelling in reverse. Designed for short distance work, the two motor carriages were put on the main line to Ballymena and soon ran themselves out, being scrapped in July 1913.

'Push-and-pull' train on the Great Northern Railway (Ireland), c 1909. These short trains, accommodating 124 passengers, were operated by a class of 4–4–0 tank locomotives of which the first three came from Beyer Peacock in the mid-1880s and ten more were built at Dundalk between 1887 and 1893. As steam rail-cars, introduced on the Great Northern in 1905, had already proved a disappointment, the widespread adoption of trains of the above type on the suburban Dublin–Howth and Belfast–Lisburn services, with the central locomotive controlled by shafts and levers from a driving compartment at either end, was a feature of the company's local train workings from this time on.

Two striking inspection vehicles on the Belfast & Northern Counties Railway, around 1900. The upper photograph is of a simple 'pedalo'-type permanent way inspector's trolley on the single track Whitehead branch: here a sound knowledge of the company's working timetable would seem to have been an essential pre-requisite for an uneventful day's work.

Below is the chief engineer's petrol-driven inspection car at York Road. Note here the back seat driver, the wicker umbrella holder and the sartorial elegance of the senior passengers.

The mechanical track-laying train designed and patented by A. W. Bretland of the Midland Great Western Railway, and in use on the Great Southern Railways from 1925, was a revolutionary advance in permanent way maintenance and was subsequently widely adopted elsewhere. Each mile of track was treated as so many units of assembled track, both as regards new track to be laid and old track to be taken up. Sections of track, already made up, were run out to the site of the re-laying on a materials train and here we see the original track layer, built by Morris of Loughborough, at work in 1927.

The Travelling Post Office of the Great Northern really dates from the introduction of the 'Limited Mails' between Dublin and Belfast in 1880, though an early postal carriage did exist on the same route from 1865. From 1880 a daily service with Post Office sorting van left Dublin at 8.15 am, Belfast at 3.15 pm. The Travelling Post Office was withdrawn from the main line in 1923, and from the Derry line in 1940.

The GNR had three Post Office sorting vans in all, at different times. Shown here is the interior of Class N2 (No 7, later No 789) built at Dundalk in 1892, a 45 ft flat-roofed bogie on service with the 'Limited Mails' on the main line.

The famous saloon carriage of William Dargan was built in 1844 by John S. Dawson, the Dublin carriage builder, presumably for use by the contractor in travelling throughout Ireland inspecting railway work in progress. Dargan presented it to the Midland Great Western Railway in 1851 and it was their State Carriage until 1903. Though new underframes and wheels were built in 1886, and the roof raised and a lavatory added in 1904, the saloon as shown here at Inchicore, redecorated in Midland blue, retains the original body of 1844. The coach was presented to the Transport Museum in Belfast by Coras Iompair Eireann and came north in the spring of 1964.

One of the special saloon carriages built in the West Clare shops at Ennis in 1906, with large windows specially designed for the tourist traffic.

One of the most remarkable carriages ever to run on Irish railways was the original first class coupé of the Waterford & Tramore Railway, which survived until 1933. Seen here at Waterford in June 1932, this carriage was built by John Dawson of Phibsborough for the opening of the line in 1853 and in its original form was probably identical with the stock supplied by Dawson for the opening of the Midland in June 1847. As described in 1852 these carriages were indeed remarkable:

... the coupé was so large and high that with the greatest of ease I could pace from side to side with my hat on... I soon discovered a sliding door by which the coupé could be divided into two chambers and on continuing my search I observed several indications of another hidden luxury which, on un-buttoning a hasp, proved to my great astonishment to be two comfortable double beds and hair mattresses in which two couples, closing the intermediate door, might separately sleep as comfortably and as innocently as if they were at home...

The influence of an earlier transport era is evident in the elegant lines of this small (23 ft 7 in) six-wheeler, which unfortunately was sold and scrapped in 1933.

A third class bogie coach of the Clogher Valley Railway, built by the Metropolitan Carriage & Waggon Co for the opening of the line in May 1887. The plain, longitudinal wooden seating of this carriage (No 17) was upholstered in 1928 and Nos 15 and 17 were also wired for electric light. Weighing 6 tons 5 cwt, 24 ft long and with an original reddish-brown livery, No 17, like all the CVR passenger coaches, had distinctive end platforms and a clerestory roof. All the coaching stock was sold by auction in 1942.

One of the fleet of six steam rail-cars built by Clayton of Lincoln which the Great Southern Railways introduced in 1928. These ugly vehicles ran on the Cork & Macroom line, on the Athlone–Sligo line and on the Harcourt Street line out of Dublin. They were not a great success and on withdrawal in 1933 the bodies passed to the Waterford & Tramore Railway as passenger coaching stock. Here No 362 is pictured at Cork on 16 September 1929.

Two unusual railway vehicles which ran for short periods in Ulster. The Londonderry Steam Road Waggon (and covered trailer) of the BCDR was ordered from the Seaham Harbour Engine Works in County Durham on 7 September 1904 and was built at a cost of £610. The railway company had ordered it to carry goods for F. King & Co of Ballyherly, near Portaferry in the Ards Peninsula, mainly to Belfast, but the steam waggon proved much too severe on the country roads of the day and it was returned to the maker in August 1905. The trailer was retained at a cost of £45.

Rail-bus No 3 of the BNCR was a converted road vehicle, an AEC petrol omnibus of 1920 which for the first six months of 1924 operated a rail service between Coleraine and Portrush, in the north of the province. It was scrapped the following year.

Three passenger carriages of the period 1890-1905 which reflect the elegant solidity of coach building at that time: (top) class A, No 400, the first Royal Saloon built by the GNR(I), was introduced into service in 1893, one of the earliest bogie coaches on the Great Northern. It was used by King Edward VII and later became the residence of a British Army Railway Transport Officer at Amiens Street from 1914 to 1922; (centre) No 471, a 45 ft first and second class non-corridor composite coach of the GS & WR, with brake compartment and lavatories, built at Inchicore in 1902; (bottom) No 83, an MGWR open third class saloon, with reversible seats, rebuilt at Broadstone in 1922 from an older third of 1902.

HEY-DAY AND DECLINE

The present century has seen a remarkable transformation in the relative importance of Irish railways as a transport medium. From a position of apparently unassailable security in the Edwardian years, in many ways the hey-day of the railway era, the next half-century witnessed a decline in prosperity and relative importance, a decline first in evidence during the years immediately following the Great War by falling receipts and decreasing traffic, and soon reflected in the withdrawal of services on peripheral lines of marginal railway working. This marginal withering slowly developed into a programme of ruthless closure and truncation until today the Irish railway network is but a fraction of its former extent. The lines which do remain, linking the main centres of population, are those with the soundest economic basis for survival, while heavy seasonal traffic on special trains provides a welcome justification for the continued existence of branch lines which otherwise might well be closed.

In the south, freight traffic in fertilisers, sugar-beet, ore, cement and oil is now of considerable importance and livestock specials from the west still cross the country to Dublin. In the north the construction of a motorway system will be linked with an integration of road and rail transport at certain points and a new station has been built at Portadown, serving much of mid-Ulster.

In retrospect it would appear that though the years from 1920 have been increasingly difficult ones for Irish railways, it was precisely the threats to survival first occurring at that time which prompted some of their finest achievements. There can be no doubt that since 1945 the country has seen a drastic withdrawal of rail services, some debatable and ill-timed, but it is now reasonable to assume that the next ten years or so, at least, will be relatively free from closures and that those lines which have survived may be developed by CIE and NIR as an integral part of national transport systems.

At the beginning of the present century the long era of railway construction was drawing to a close. Shown here and on the next page is work in progress on the viaduct across the river Callan at Ballyards, on the Armagh–Keady section of the Castleblayney Keady & Armagh Railway, opened on 31 May 1909.

At many other places the introduction of new building materials and constructional techniques, coupled with a reappraisal and subsequent readjustment of short sections of railway in the light of continuing physical difficulties (Bray Head realignment), traffic fluctuations (the gradual singling of parts of the Derry Road) or even of factors only remotely connected with rail transport itself (the construction of the Bleach Green viaducts at Whiteabbey), resulted in a number of interesting schemes of which the two

illustrated here are perhaps less well known than most. In 1910-11 Breen Bridge spanning the Mourne at Victoria Bridge, County Tyrone, was rebuilt and the existing cast-iron girder trellis replaced by an enclosed trough of riveted sheets; secondly, at Strabane itself, the construction of the Mourne Bridge in 1911 saw a realignment of the track on the 'up' side of the station there and a shifting of the South Cabin to the position east of the track, which it occupied until the line closed in February 1965.

The following year saw the introduction of the larger and more powerful 'Q' class engines of the GNR (I) on the Derry Road, a development made possible by preparatory civil engineering work, as outlined here.

This was very much the hey-day of the Irish railway system, with no foreseeable threat to the supremacy of the steam train for comfortable, long distance travel. Though faster schedules were certainly introduced somewhat later, with larger, more powerful engines hauling heavier trains, this was something of a final fling made in the face of increasing operational difficulties and for various reasons such developments were not sustained for any length of time.

Seen here in a proudly posed picture at Amiens Street, Dublin, around 1900, is the 'main line corridor express' headed by locomotive No 135, **Cyclops**, a 'Q' class 4–4–0 built by Neilson Reid in 1899, one of thirteen such engines built for the Great Northern between 1899 and 1904 to Charles Clifford's design to handle the 'Limited Mails' between Dublin and Belfast. Train catering started on the GNR in 1895 and one of the early dining saloons is second from the front here.

Soon, however, in areas of short haul traffic, around Belfast and Dublin in particular, a novel means of travel made its presence felt. The earliest road vehicles driven by the internal combustion engine, in their rickety appearance and temperamental running scarcely bearing comparison with the proven solidity and strength of the steam train, were in fact the thin end of a wedge which within little over forty years was to shatter the monopoly enjoyed by the railways in handling short distance commuter and excursion traffic, and force many of them to close down. The view at the foot of the opposite page shows the street approaches to the Bangor station of the BCDR around 1910.

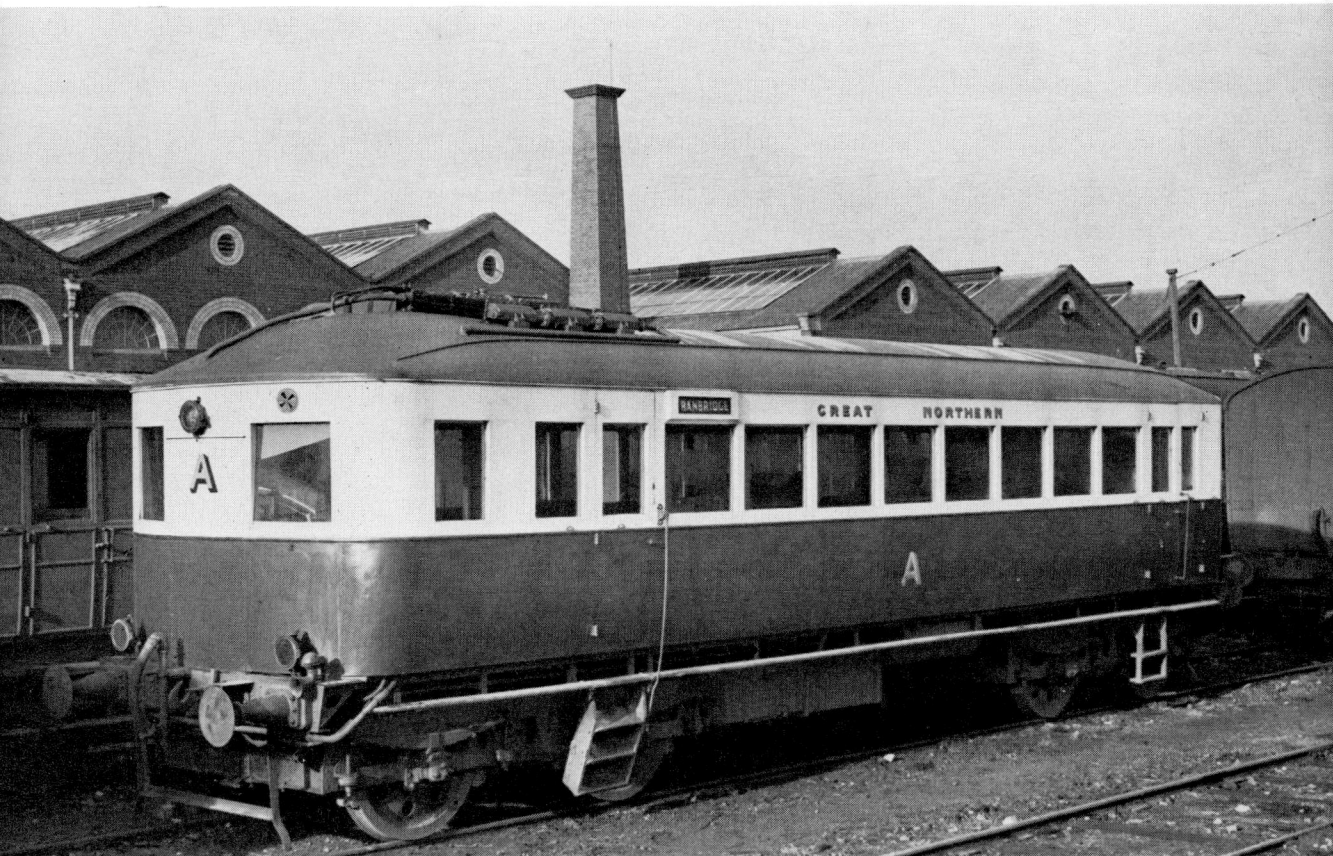

In an attempt to effect economy in the working of railways through the sparsely populated areas of County Donegal, the County Donegal Railways Joint Committee in the 1920s introduced rail-buses, road vehicles converted to run on permanent way. The idea soon spread to the broad-gauge Great Northern system, part owners of the narrow-gauge network, and perhaps more than any other railway company in the British Isles the GNR (I) pioneered the introduction and successful operation of diesel traction on rails, with a fleet of rail-buses and rail-cars providing services on many minor branch lines where light traffic made full steam working unprofitable.

Rail-car A was a diesel mechanical car with a 130 hp AEC six-cylinder heavy oil engine built at Dundalk in 1932. It worked mainly from Portadown and had seats for thirty-two persons, a top speed of 50 mph, fuel consumption 8-10 mpg and an operational cost of around 4d per mile. This pioneer vehicle ran successfully for over thirty years and its success prompted the construction of a whole fleet of rail-cars and buses. Somewhat ironically, in 1964 rail-car A was sold by the Ulster Transport Authority to a contractor and was used subsequently in the lifting of the Navan–Clonsilla branch of the former MGWR (1964) and, latterly, of the Derry Road (1966-7).

In the south an equally enterprising development was occurring at this time in the introduction of the Drumm Battery Trains on the Great Southern Railways. Dr James Drumm of Dublin developed a low resistance alkaline battery for which an efficiency of 75 per cent on tractive purposes was claimed. Charging was necessary on the basis of one minute for each mile run and the capacity of the battery allowed 90–100 miles running between charges. Following successful tests on a converted Drewry petrol rail-car, the first two new rail-car sets powered by the Drumm battery entered service in 1931-2 on the Dublin–Bray–Greystones route, with occasional runs out as far as Wicklow. During World War II the four 'Drumms', as they were universally known, provided almost the entire suburban service between Dublin and Bray. They were withdrawn in 1949 when the batteries became due for renewal and the coaches were converted to ordinary passenger stock. Seen here at Wicklow station on its first run in October 1932 is rail-car B of the Drumm Battery fleet.

By the mid 1930s it was becoming apparent on certain sections of the northern railway system that even the rail-cars already in service were too large for the traffic available and George B. Howden, chief civil and locomotive engineer of the Great Northern, collaborated with a fellow engineer at Dundalk to produce the remarkable Howden-Meredith wheel, which greatly facilitated the conversion of conventional road buses for use on the railways. The wheel had a steel rim or tyre between the pneumatic tyre and the rail surface and within a few months of successful trials on the Omagh–Derry line in 1934 a number of these rail-buses came from the Dundalk shops, including two for the Dundalk Newry & Greenore Railway Company. In the late 1930s these two buses usually covered between 15,000 and 20,000 miles annually. Seen here at Greenore in August 1935 is No 1, which was transferred back to the Great Northern in 1947 and finally withdrawn and scrapped in 1955.

The early 1930s saw the completion of two major schemes of civil engineering on Irish railways, the reconstruction of the Boyne viaduct at Drogheda and the building of a new 'loop line' between Whiteabbey and Monkstown on the Northern Counties main line to Londonderry.

At Drogheda the old structure, opened in 1855 as a continuous girder bridge, was replaced by three simply supported spans of similar length, resting on the original masonry piers. The viaduct had carried double track but as only one train had been allowed on the bridge at a time since around 1885, it was decided to design the new structure to carry a double line, but with interlaced track. The work was carried out between 1930 and 1932 under the supervision of George B. Howden, without interruption of traffic: the old track was singled and the new steel girders placed between the rails and the old bridge, as illustrated here. This major rebuilding paved the way for the introduction of the powerful compound locomotives, with heavier axle load, and consequently of faster main line services between Dublin and Belfast.

The Greenisland 'loop line' between Belfast and Antrim, built between 1931 and 1934, is an avoiding line 2¾ miles in length which enabled main line trains to run straight through, to and from Belfast, without the necessity of running out to Greenisland on the Larne branch and reversing up to Monkstown on the main line, as hitherto. An arrangement was reached between the Government of Northern Ireland and the Directors of the Northern Counties for the construction of the loop as an unemployment relief scheme and work began in 1931. At its southern end the scheme involved the construction of two large reinforced concrete viaducts spanning Valentine's Glen, of which the larger, carrying the main double track on a continuous curve, is 630 ft long and has a maximum height of 70 ft above the stream. The main line viaduct was built in eighteen months and 'down' trains on the Larne line pass underneath the main line in a 'burrowing junction' before crossing the glen on a separate viaduct. The two viaducts and the undercrossing required 17,000 cu yd of concrete and 700 tons of mild steel reinforcement, at a total cost of around £65,000. This was the last major scheme of civil engineering carried out on Irish railways.

Seen here are the main (left) and shore line viaducts under construction in March 1933, looking north from directly above the burrowing junction.

Locomotive building, assembly and repair continued at Inchicore, Dundalk and York Road all through the 1930s and here we see an 0–6–0 mixed traffic engine (GN class 'UG') being built at the Dundalk shops in March 1937, one of five such locomotives built there at that time to a design by H. R. McIntosh.

As we have seen, on the Great Northern the 1930s saw the introduction of very fast schedules on main line workings; so, too, on the Northern Counties system the arrival of the 'Moguls' in 1933 and the completion of the Greenisland loop in the following year were a prelude to the speeding up of certain services and the introduction of several named 'specials', of which the 'Portrush Flyer', the 'Golfers' Express' and the 'North Atlantic Express' were the most famous. By 1937 the timing for the Portrush–Belfast run (67.6 miles) had been reduced to 74 minutes, inclusive of a stop at Ballymena, and here the 'up' Portrush Flyer, with Mogul No 95, **The Braid**, and consisting of twelve full bogies, leaves Portrush on a July evening in that year.

The peak of locomotive building in Ireland was undoubtedly marked by the construction of the three '800' class three-cylinder 4–6–0 express passenger locomotives for the Great Southern Railways. Designed by E. C. Bredin and built at Inchicore on the eve of World War II these engines were numbered 800, 801 and 802 and named **Maeve**, **Macha** and **Tailte**. They were the most powerful express locomotives ever built for an Irish railway. The three cylinders had a diameter of $18\frac{1}{2}$ in and a stroke of 28 in, the driving wheels were 6 ft 7 in in diameter, the boiler pressure 225 psi and the tractive effort 34,780 lb. The combined weight of locomotive and tender was 135 tons and the length, over buffers, 67 ft 9 in.

Unfortunately these fine locomotives were given little opportunity to prove themselves fully in service, and in post-war years, with fuel difficulties and a general policy of dieselisation, they were withdrawn from regular passenger service in 1955. No 800, **Maeve**, is now in the Ulster Transport Museum; the other two engines were scrapped, No 802 in 1957, No 801 in 1963.

Here No 802, **Tailte**, passes through Straffan in July 1948, on a Cork–Dublin Sunday working, the first regular Sunday main line train after World War II.

The German air raids of the nights of 15/16 April and 4/5 May 1941 severely damaged the York Road terminus of the LMS (NCC) in Belfast and, besides the damage to buildings, the vast majority of civil and mechanical engineering drawings, and many valuable manuscript and documentary records were destroyed.

During the 1939-45 war the 'border' between Northern Ireland and the Irish Republic assumed an added, commercial significance and gave a new meaning to Customs examinations at Goraghwood, Tynan, Strabane and Belcoo stations. The Great Northern took advantage of its position astride the political boundary and ran shopping specials to places like Dundalk, Clones, Cavan and Monaghan. These services were well patronised by housewives anxious to supplement the meagre official 'rations' of war-time Ulster and by husbands quick to appreciate the differential between licensed trade prices, north and south. Here a trainload of shoppers from Belfast arrives at Cavan.

The war affected the railways in other ways, too. For example, the aerodrome at Aldergrove, close to the Knockmore Junction–Antrim branch of the Great Northern, expanded greatly and a large aircraft assembly and repair depot was set up close by at Gortnagallon. In May 1942, a $2\frac{1}{4}$ mile siding was opened from the Antrim branch and throughout the remainder of the war thousands of workers were conveyed to and from Belfast in special trains, under somewhat Spartan conditions. Here an early morning workers' train has just arrived at Gortnagallon in August 1943.

On the Northern Counties section of the LMS the end of the war saw the overall position as regards locomotive maintenance and overhaul little short of desperate and it was decided to ask Harland & Wolff to undertake the overhaul of some of the Mogul engines. Accordingly, in 1945-6, nine of these locomotives were sent in turn along the Albert Quay and taken across the river by the shipyard's 200 ton floating crane for complete overhaul.

The immediate post war years saw the last steam locomotives appearing on the Irish railway scene. No conventional steam engines were built at Inchicore after the '800' class of 1939 and it was in the north, on the Great Northern, Northern Counties and Sligo Leitrim systems that the new arrivals appeared between 1946 and 1951.

One of the most interesting groups was the 'VS' class of the GNR, a batch of five three-cylinder simple 4–4–0s built by Beyer Peacock in 1948 for main line passenger work. H. R. McIntosh's design bore many similarities to Glover's compounds of 1932 and it will be noted that here again the Great Northern favoured a 4–4–0 wheel arrangement for passenger express locomotives, an arrangement largely dictated by the dimensions of the Dundalk shops. These 'VS' engines were the last 4–4–0 locomotives ever built and the last steam engines put into service on the Great Northern system. They were named after Irish rivers and numbered 206-210. The last of the class remained in use until the final eclipse of steam in the mid-1960s.

Here we see a Dundalk draughtsman working on the 'VS' design in 1947 with, below, the last survivor of the class, No 207, **Boyne**, approaching Adavoyle up the bank from Dundalk on a 'down' main line special, 20 April 1964.

In the south the severe coal shortage of the immediate post-war years saw the conversion of over ninety steam locomotives to oil burning between 1945 and 1948. The burner itself, a simple device fitted at the front of each fire box, was made entirely at Inchicore. These oil burners proved quite satisfactory in service but with the easing of the fuel shortage early in 1948 all were reconverted for normal coal consumption. A large white circle on tender and/or smoke box door indicated to signalmen that the train was being hauled by an oil burner and was to be given preference over a coal burning engine.

Here CIE locomotive No 601, an 0–6–0 built at the Broadstone shops in 1888 as MGWR No 62, **Tiger**, is seen as an oil burner at Edenderry on a Gaelic Athletic Association special on St Patrick's Day 1948.

The fuel shortage is further reflected in this view of a turf train for Dublin approaching Portarlington along the Athlone branch, with a large part of the train consisting of old six-wheeled passenger stock, windows boarded up and roofs removed.

In August 1947, for the first time, with the inauguration of the Great Northern 'Enterprise Express' between Belfast and Dublin, the Irish time-tables showed a regular booked run of over 100 miles non-stop. This was made possible by arranging for the Customs examinations to be carried out before departure or on arrival. The train comprised seven coaches—a third class brake, two thirds, a buffet car, two firsts and another third class brake—and accommodation was provided for 72 first and 200 third class passengers. The original 'Enterprise' left Belfast at 10.30 am and Dublin at 5.30 pm, the time allowed in each direction being $2\frac{1}{4}$ hours for 112.6 miles.

Here the original Dublin–Belfast 'Enterprise Express', headed by locomotive No 83, **Eagle**, crosses the Craigmore viaduct on the evening of 11 August 1947.

From October 1950 until June 1953 the 'Enterprise Express' ran through to Cork. In this working the entire train of the 10.30 am 'up' service from Belfast was hauled from Amiens Street by a CIE locomotive of the '800' or '400' class, leaving at 1.30 pm, 45 minutes after its scheduled arrival from the north. The 'up' express from Cork left at 1.15 pm, called at Limerick Junction for a seven minute stop, and arrived at Amiens Street at 4.45 pm, leaving for Belfast 45 minutes later.

Shown here at Limerick Junction on the Cork–Dublin 'Enterprise' of 24 August 1952, is locomotive No 402, built to E. A. Watson's design at Inchicore in 1920-1, with four cylinders and 6 ft 7 in driving wheels, and rebuilt by his successor, J. R. Bazin, in 1927 with two cylinders, new frames, cylinders, motion and wheels. This 'B2' class 4–6–0, withdrawn in 1961, still holds the record for the Cork–Dublin run, 165.4 miles in 147 minutes. This run, with the American ambassador's train on 30 March 1934, was done with three bogie coaches weighing 93 tons and is all the more remarkable when one remembers that it included two slacks, one of 10 mph, the other of 40 mph, between Mallow and Limerick Junction.

Despite the various developments noted on the previous pages the post-war era was one of increasing difficulty for Irish railways, culminating in the widespread withdrawal of steam traction, the closure of large portions of the railway network and the streamlining of main line workings into a skeleton service of modern diesel-electric trains. The two photographs here tell their own sad story: (top) a row of Ulster Transport Authority locomotives, mainly old BCDR stock, awaits the auctioneer's hammer at Queen's Quay in January 1956, while (below) the last of the Woolwich locomotives of CIE (No 388) is cut up at Mullingar in April 1963.

ULSTER TRANSPORT AUTHORITY
GREAT NORTHERN RAILWAY BOARD
CORAS IOMPAIR EIREANN
ERNE BUS SERVICE

WITHDRAWAL OF RAIL SERVICES

Portadown—Armagh—
Monaghan—Clones—Cavan
Ballyhaise—Belturbet
Omagh—Enniskillen—Clones—Dundalk
Fintona Junction—Fintona
Bundoran Junction—Bundoran
Enniskillen—Sligo

TIME TABLE
OF
Alternative Road Services
(Including Rail connections at Portadown, Omagh and Dundalk)
FROM
Monday, 14th October, 1957
SUBJECT TO ALTERATION

The withdrawal of services was followed fairly promptly by track lifting. One of the most severe truncations of the Irish railway system occurred in the autumn of 1957 when a major programme of closures was applied at one fell swoop and the greater part of west Ulster was left without rail services for the first time for upwards of seventy-five years.

Because of the terrorist activity at that time being directed, *inter alia*, against the Ulster railway system, the Ulster Transport Authority wasted no time in removing potential targets for IRA attacks and the lower picture shows the demolition of the Blackwater bridge on the Armagh–Monaghan section of the former Great Northern system.

One aspect of the railway network which has been an increasing headache for road authorities in recent years of expanding traffic was the road hazard constituted by the familiar pattern of road crossing rail by an overbridge, necessitating an abrupt change of direction on the part of road traffic moving in either direction. To avoid accentuating the costly 'skew' archway at the time the railway was built, the bridge frequently incorporated only a slight angle of traverse. In the past half century it was often a serious hazard to the increasing traffic on trunk roads, and was difficult to rebuild without interruption to road and rail. As was the case on the main Omagh–Londonderry road near Mountjoy in County Tyrone, as soon as rail traffic was withdrawn in February 1965 a bridge of this type, carrying a trunk route with heavy commercial traffic, was rebuilt almost immediately.

The closing months of 1966 saw the end of steam workings on the Great Northern section of the Ulster Transport Authority, some $3\frac{1}{2}$ years after Coras Iompair Eireann had finally transferred their entire tractive power from steam to diesel, and the UTA organised a special enthusiasts' excursion from Belfast to Dublin and back, on 29 October 1966, to commemorate 111 years of steam operation on that route. As no suitable ex-GNR locomotive had survived in the UTA fleet an ex-NCC 'Jeep' or 2–6–4T, No 54, worked the special, an assorted rake of eight carriages, all ex-Great Northern stock, and the train is shown here passing through Adelaide on the southbound journey.

On abandoned lines what has happened to the stations which were for many years the centre of bustle and activity and an integral part of the life of numerous country towns? Like Enniskillen, County Fermanagh (top) which is now completely demolished, most suffered badly at the hands of vandals and were soon reduced to desolate wastes of rotting plaster, decaying timbers, smashed glass and corroding ironwork; others, much less numerous, were successfully adapted to new purposes, as at Limavady, County Londonderry, where the former station has been used as a 'bus terminus (centre) or at Victoria Road, in Londonderry itself (bottom) where a progressive wholesaler has roofed in the platforms of the former narrow-gauge station for storage purposes, and uses the station building itself as an administrative office block.

RECENT DEVELOPMENTS

A two-fold trend can be distinguished on Irish railways in recent years—dieselisation, accompanied by a pruning and streamlining of main line services to a standard and frequency in keeping with the traffic requirements of today and, secondly, the widespread closure of unremunerative branch lines. In the south, steam finally gave way to diesel-electric traction in the spring of 1963; in the north, apart from outings organised by railway enthusiasts and shunting at York Road, steam working in recent years has been restricted to the occasional specials to Portrush and Londonderry in the summer months, together with 'spoil' traffic and the odd service train on the Larne branch, all is in the hands of the surviving post-war 'WT' class tanks.

Fast inter-city diesel-electrics link Dublin with Belfast, Cork and Galway, and the services to Sligo, Waterford and Londonderry have been greatly improved of late. Because of the nature of the services, and the enforced speed restrictions on many lines, the post-war years have not been characterised by record runs, which belong rather to another age when such performances had their uses in boosting the public image of particular companies and services. The railways which remain have had to adjust themselves to changing circumstances, more specifically to the staggering increase in the number of vehicles, both private and commercial, flooding on to Irish roads year by year. They have by now accepted and digested this fact and have geared many of their services and facilities to ensure survival in the face of increasing competition from road traffic. In the Belfast and Dublin areas growing traffic congestion on the roads and the introduction of parking meters in the down-town zones have given the railways an opportunity they have not been slow to seize, while in the south major reconstructional schemes at Dun Laoghaire, Rosslare and Limerick Junction have greatly facilitated the travelling public. Mineral exploitation has resulted in branch line construction in Counties Limerick and Tipperary, while there is a substantial traffic in oil, beet, turf, coal, fertilisers, feeding stuffs, cement and livestock. In Ulster the programme of motorway construction, besides providing a direct traffic on the Larne branch, is being implemented in such a way as to suggest an integration of road and rail transport facilities and the Government at Stormont has recently indicated its intention of encouraging the new statutory body, Northern Ireland Railways, to develop its services over the next ten years as part of the new and progressive image of the province.

In 1955 the change-over from steam to diesel-electric traction on Coras Iompair Eireann began in earnest, and in that year ninety-four diesel-electric mixed traffic locomotives were ordered from Metropolitan Vickers Electrical Co Ltd. Delivery began in July and here one of these early diesel-electrics, with Co-Co wheel formation and driven by a Crossley engine developing 1,200 bhp, passes Killiney in June 1956.

(Right) In 1961 the first fifteen engines of a new fleet of American diesel-electrics were introduced and in the following year an additional thirty-seven of these General Motors locomotives (B141-B177) were brought over, each 'double ended' and of Bo-Bo wheel formation. These locomotives were soon handling most of CIE's passenger and freight traffic, often running in pairs on heavy trains, and here B168 passes Killiney in July 1963 on the Dublin–Bray line of the former Dublin & South Eastern Railway Company.

In the north, too, though not undertaken in quite such a workmanlike fashion, steam has been gradually replaced by diesel or diesel-electric traction from the end of World War II onwards. In 1948 the Great Northern decided to purchase twenty diesel rail-cars from AEC Ltd of Southall and to introduce them on both main and branch line workings. Each diesel car had a power output of 250 bhp and the idea was to run a standard coach between two powered units, providing seating accommodation for 142 passengers. The livery was royal blue, with cream upper panels and grey roof, and these AEC rail-cars, numbered from 600 to 619 inclusive, performed well over the extensive Great Northern system and were not joined by the next diesel units until 1957.

Here four of these early AEC diesel rail-car sets are seen at Great Victoria Street, Belfast, soon after they had entered service in 1948.

Early in 1955 an 800 hp diesel-hydraulic locomotive with 0–D–0 wheel arrangement, built in Kiel, was introduced on the Great Northern system, mainly for handling freight traffic on the main and Derry lines. Though quite successful this locomotive (opposite, above) seen on the main line near Dunmurry, County Antrim, was the sole example of its type. It passed to CIE in 1958 and at the time of going to press remains in service at Cork, though little used.

Introduced on the Belfast–Dublin service on 4 July 1970 the new 'Enterprise' of Northern Ireland Railways marks the culmination of a two-year development programme costing around £¾ million and may be regarded as something of an investment by the Northern Ireland Government in the future of Irish rail transport.

Making two journeys each way daily in 2 hrs 10 mins the eight-coach train is powered by two diesel-electric locomotives of 1,350 hp each, supplied by the Hunslet Engine Co Ltd of Leeds and built at Doncaster. Three locomotives in all have been ordered, **Eagle**, **Falcon** and **Merlin**, which names perpetuate G. T. Glover's historic three-cylinder compounds of the early 1930s, one of the most noteworthy classes ever to run between Dublin and Belfast.

The two locomotives drive from both ends simultaneously, permitting speedy turn-arounds and giving greater power over the bank between Goraghwood and Dundalk.

The train itself incorporates many novel features in Irish rail travel, all contributing to maximum passenger comfort, and is one of the most important advances yet made by Northern Ireland Railways towards re-establishing inter-city rail travel at a time of steadily increasing road congestion.

Seen here on the 'up' 2.30 pm working at Great Victoria Street, Belfast, on 6 July 1970, is locomotive 102, **Falcon**, which with **Eagle** had made the inaugural run three days previously. The train is finished in a striking maroon and blue livery; the locomotives are maroon and yellow.

Early in 1952 locomotive No 356 of CIE was experimentally converted at Inchicore to burn turf or oil (top) and following exhaustive tests on this prototype a turf-burning locomotive (bottom) was built to the design of O. V. S. Bulleid, then consulting mechanical engineer with CIE. This closely guarded locomotive design first appeared in August 1957 but though trial runs were made on the main line to Cork, the subsequent duties of the turf burner were mainly between Kingsbridge and North Wall. The 0–6–6–0 tank locomotive was withdrawn in 1965.

The end of the Great Northern Railway Board in 1958 saw a division of locomotive power between CIE and UTA. Locomotive No 207, **Boyne**, a 'VS' class 4–4–0 in service with the GNR since 1948, went south but was rebought by the UTA in June 1963 when steam traction ceased in the Republic. Photographed here at Adelaide in June 1964, still with its CIE lettering, this engine was the last of the 'VS's to be scrapped, being withdrawn in December 1965.

A 'down' line MED rail-car set in NIR grey and maroon livery, stops at Seahill halt on the Belfast–Bangor line between Marino and Helen's Bay in December 1968. This halt was opened to traffic on 4 April 1966 and was built in direct response to the potential commuter traffic created by an influx of population to new housing development in the area along the south shore of Belfast Lough, some eight miles from the city.

One of several automatic continental-type road crossings now in operation on Northern Ireland Railways, at Lissue, near Lisburn, County Antrim, on the main Belfast–Portadown–Dublin line.

One of the most interesting developments on Irish railways in recent years was the creation of a heavy traffic in 'spoil' on the Larne branch of Northern Ireland Railways, a traffic which began in December 1966 and ceased in May 1970. The spoil (quarry waste) was drawn from Magheramorne on the shore of Larne Lough, to the foreshore of Belfast Lough just outside the city, where it was tipped out at new sidings as motorway filling. At the outset these trains ran five times in each direction daily, each train consisting of eight or ten waggons, but with a revision of timetables at the beginning of 1967 the number of trains was reduced and their length increased. Shown here is a train of twenty of the special four-wheeled hoppers on the 'up' line at Whitehead on 9 August 1968, with 'Jeeps' 53 and 5 working hard fore and aft.

RECORDING AND PRESERVATION

It is paradoxical but hardly surprising that the eclipse of steam and the closure of many branch lines has resulted in a great increase in public interest in Irish railways. In nearly every country railways have long been a source of great interest for a relatively small band of devotees, drawn from all walks of life and from all age groups, and Ireland has proved no exception. In the immediate post-war years this corporate feeling crystallised in the formation of the Irish Railway Record Society in Dublin, and this body has gone from strength to strength ever since, encouraging the study of Irish railways, organising numerous outings over many sections of the Irish railway network, publishing railway material from a wide range of interests and actively commenting on and reporting the changing Irish railway scene. The library of the society, now housed in new premises in Dublin, contains the finest collection of specialised railway publications in Ireland, and members of the society have done much valuable work in securing and cataloguing various collections of photographs, engineering drawings and miscellaneous railway material which would otherwise have been destroyed in the organisation and modernisation of the last twenty years.

More recently, in September 1964, a second society, the Railway Preservation Society of Ireland, has been formed in the north and, while somewhat different in their aims and objects, the two bodies now work closely together. The RPSI owns two steam locomotives, has an option to purchase a third at present leased from Northern Ireland Railways, and has recently launched an appeal to rescue a fourth, still in service. These are normally kept at Whitehead, County Antrim, and the society aims to maintain its locomotives in such a way as to be able to run several outings with them each year over various parts of the Irish railway network. It has no plans to acquire a stretch of line, nor any hope of raising the funds to do so; neither would it presume to have the manpower or technical knowledge which the use of this would entail. Its main intention is to restore and maintain in working order several fine examples of Irish steam locomotives of the past, together with coaches and other items of railway equipment.

The Belfast society is well represented in the Dublin area and the IRRS has Belfast, Cork (Munster) and London area branches.

In addition to the above, recent developments in industrial archaeology, particularly in Ulster, have ensured that the remains of the railway network are studied and recorded as part of official programmes of research and fieldwork. In the north this work has been carried out under the aegis of the Ministry of Finance in the Government of Northern Ireland; in the south as part of a broad inventory of the national heritage drawn up by the National Institute for Physical Planning and Construction Research. In Ulster such work has been greatly assisted by the successful efforts of the Public Record Office in Belfast where a considerable tonnage of documentary material relating to north Irish railways is now available for consultation. In Dublin a large volume of comparable material with Coras Iompair Eireann is held in the muniment rooms at Connolly and Heuston Stations and may be freely inspected by prior arrangement with the secretary's office.

In Belfast is to be found Ireland's only public Transport Museum, an institution now forming part of the Ulster Folk Museum but originating in the foresight of a small group of enthusiasts on Belfast Corporation who, as early as 1954, gained official recognition for their efforts by establishing a prototype store/museum as an offshoot of the Belfast Museum and Art Gallery. From this has developed the present collection of transport relics from all over the country, including a substantial section devoted to Irish railways.

Finally, it is worth noting that while no comparable institution exists in the Republic, Coras Iompair Eireann have been most helpful in ensuring that the Belfast collection is as representative of the whole of the country as possible, and have also kindly agreed to preserve, restore and exhibit several Irish locomotives of outstanding historical significance at various points on their railway network. No 184 has already been restored to working order at Inchicore, No 36 is on display at Cork, No 90 at Mallow and No 5 at Ennis; plans are also afoot to restore and display No 461 at Wexford and No 131 at Dundalk.

One of the features of the contraction of the Irish railway system has been the various enthusiasts' specials organised by the Irish Railway Record Society and the Railway Preservation Society of Ireland on lines over which the axe was poised. Seen here at Courtmacsherry is the IRRS outing on the Timoleague & Courtmacsherry Railway, run on 20 August 1960, and patronised by over seventy members. For this trip 0–6–0T No 90, withdrawn from service in October 1959, was specially resurrected to work the Ballinascarthy–Courtmacsherry section.

This little engine is worthy of particular attention. Built at Inchicore in 1875 as an 0–6–4T, one of Alexander McDonnell's light locomotives with carriage portion over the trailing bogie, the engine was rebuilt in 1915 as an 0–6–0 side tank and worked on the Timoleague & Courtmacsherry line for many years, until 1954. CIE kindly agreed to No 90 being stationed on the back platform at Mallow, fully lined out in GS & WR livery, as a permanent reminder of one aspect of Irish railway history.

On 9 September 1967 an outing organised by the Railway Preservation Society of Ireland travelled from York Road, Belfast, to Dundalk (Barrack Street) and back. The motive power here was provided by locomotive No 186, an 0–6–0 of the famous 'J15' class which was presented to the RPSI by Coras Iompair Eireann in 1965 and is now stationed at Whitehead. The train is seen here on the 'up' line at Goraghwood.

At Kent Station, formerly Glanmire Road, Cork, is preserved a 2–2–2 locomotive built by Bury Curtis & Kennedy of Liverpool in 1848 for the Great Southern & Western Railway Co of Ireland. Withdrawn in 1875 after logging almost half a million miles of main line working, this historic locomotive was repaired, painted and transferred to Cork in November 1950 where a section of the original GS & WR permanent way—90 lb iron bridge rails on cross sleepers—was reconstructed under cover on the station platform. When originally laid in 1846-9 these rails were by far the heaviest in the world. No 36, seen here at Inchicore at the time of the transfer to Cork, has 6 ft driving wheels and weighs 22 tons 19 cwt.

On 12 May 1962 a suburban outing in open waggons, organised jointly by the Irish Railway Record Society and the former Northern Ireland Road & Rail Development Association, ran over the Belfast Central Railway, hauled by an 0–6–4 tank locomotive of the Great Northern 'RT' class. The train is here seen moving towards Maysfields, having just crossed the Lagan Bridge, with, on the right, the line which formerly led to Donegall Quay through a tunnel passing beneath the Queen's Bridge.

The Transport Museum, in Belfast, has recently passed from the control of a municipal authority (Belfast Corporation) and is now a part of the Ulster Folk Museum at Cultra, some 5 miles outside the city, whence it will be moved as soon as practicable. Having its origins in the enthusiasm of a small group of Corporation members, the museum was officially opened in 1962 and houses a remarkable collection of transport relics, including four broad-gauge locomotives and a representative selection of narrow-gauge engines, tramcars and rolling stock from all over Ireland. Many items held in store cannot be displayed for lack of space but it is hoped that the museum's new surroundings, a wooded estate flanking the Bangor branch of the former Belfast & County Down Railway, will allow proper display and facilitate locomotive workings.

Seen here in the present museum building at Witham Street, Belfast, is the locomotive **Blanche** of the former County Donegal narrow-gauge system with, on the right, Electric Car No 2 of the former Bessbrook & Newry Tramway and, immediately behind the engine, a directors' saloon of the County Donegal Railway Company, built in 1882.

The marshalling of exhibits for the Transport Museum more often than not resolves itself into a question of securing unique items before they are sold for scrap or broken up by firms, companies or authorities when their working life comes to an end. Seen here at Londonderry in November 1964, being run on to a low loader for road transfer to Belfast, is locomotive No 1 of the Londonderry Port & Harbour Commissioners, an 0–6–0 saddle tank built by Robert Stephenson & Co Ltd of Newcastle-upon-Tyne in 1891 for shunting work along the Derry quays on both sides of the river. The dock sidings were originally of mixed gauge (5 ft 3 in and 3 ft) and while the Harbour Commissioners' engines were of 5 ft 3 in gauge they could be coupled to waggons of either gauge, with trains of mixed-gauge stock a common sight.

The demise of steam on southern Irish railways in the spring of 1963 was followed in February 1964 by the transfer to Belfast of the last of the three '800' class locomotives built at Inchicore in 1939, along with William Dargan's saloon. No 800, **Maeve**, is seen here being eased into the Transport Museum on a winter morning in November 1964, a photograph which surely epitomises the transient nature of our technological environment where scientific invention and progress make mockery of the brilliant ideas and engineering skills of the previous generation.

ACKNOWLEDGMENTS AND SOURCES

To compress the long and eventful history of Irish railways within the bounds of a single work seemed at first an impossible task. Irish railways have long been a subject of especial interest to enthusiasts and tourists from all over Europe and beyond, and there existed an enormous pool of photographs from which to select a representative cross-section. Furthermore, how could one person feel qualified to make such a broad selection, to tell such an absorbing story, in a field where expertise and specialised knowledge on countless minutiae of railway history, locomotive development and train working abound?

Inevitably a book of this nature is bound to be dependent to a large degree on the advice and help of others, and to Mr R. N. Clements of Celbridge, County Kildare, I owe a particular debt of gratitude. His knowledge of Irish railways, particularly of locomotive development and company workings, is unrivalled and from a great depth of first-hand experience, extending over forty years, he answered my countless queries with unfailing courtesy and patience and was most liberal in providing me with both information and illustrative material.

The very large number of others who gave of their time to assist me, or who lent me photographs from their private collections, include, in Dublin, Messrs George Mahon, Patrick Flanagan, Kevin Murray, Herbert Richards, Alan Newham, P. J. Currivan and Lyal Collen and, in Belfast, Messrs William Robb, Maurice Batley, Noel Craig, Alfred Montgomery and Drew Donaldson. Mr Harold Houston of Whitehead, County Antrim, and Mr Walter McGrath of Cork provided many items of outstanding interest for my perusal while Mrs Bretland of Malahide and Messrs Duffner of Dundalk, Coakham and Liddle of Bangor, Clendinning of Lurgan and Weatherup and FitzGerald of Armagh were more than kind in their patient co-operation and assistance. The Rector of St Mary's, Port Laois, kindly granted me freedom of access to the collection of the late Father Browne while Dr Gillespie of Ballygawley, County Tyrone, provided original photographs and first-hand information on the Clogher Valley Railway.

In Great Britain, Mr Henry Casserley of Berkhamsted placed his unique collection of photographs at my disposal while Dr Edward Patterson of West Kilbride in Ayrshire, Mr Lance King of Harrow, Mr L. G. Marshall of Crawley and Mr W. A. Camwell of Birmingham answered specific requests for particular items.

Of the large number of institutions and public bodies which I had occasion to visit or contact I am particularly grateful to the Director and staff of the National Library of Ireland, in Dublin, for their assistance in enabling me to work in depth on the Lawrence and Eason collections of negatives. The Welch collection at the Ulster Museum, Belfast, and the Green collection of the Ulster Folk Museum also provided material of interest, and I am grateful to the Directors and staff of these institutions for full co-operation in my researches. Similarly the staff of the Transport Museum in Belfast contributed a wide range of material from their miscellaneous files on railway subjects. The Cooper collection of photographs in the Public Record Office, Northern Ireland, contains many railway items hitherto unpublished and my sincere thanks are due here to the Deputy Keeper and his staff for full facilities in inspecting and selecting material, and to Mr H. D. H. Cooper of Strabane, County Tyrone, for permission to reproduce several of these. The Central Lending Library in Belfast holds a large number of photographs, and a quantity of miscellaneous material relating to Irish railways, particularly the GNR (I), and here again the sub-librarian in charge of the Irish section granted full facilities for inspection. As ever, the Linenhall Library in Belfast proved an invaluable source of reference on countless occasions and to Mr James Vitty and his staff an especial debt of gratitude is due for co-operation and assistance far beyond that normally expected from a large subscribers' library. The Ministry of Finance in the Government of Northern Ireland kindly granted permission for the reproduction of photographs taken by the author during the course of the Survey of Industrial Archaeology.

Coras Iompair Eireann, the British Science Museum, the Birmingham Central Reference Library, the Electricity Supply Board in Dublin, the Institution of Civil Engineers of Ireland, Trinity College Dublin, the Irish Railway Record Society, the Queen's University of Belfast, the Belfast Water Commissioners,

Armagh County Museum, the Railway Preservation Society of Ireland, Arthur Guinness Son & Co Ltd, the Board of Public Works and the Public Record Office, Ireland, all these supplied information and/or material and without their help the book would have been the poorer.

A book of this nature of necessity involves a great deal of technical skill in the printing of indifferent negatives or in the resuscitation of old, faded prints, many of them over eighty years of age, by careful copying. The preparation of a wide range of material for the publisher, both line and half-tone, has been a task requiring great technical expertise and individual craftsmanship of a high order, and in this Mr Lionel Salem of the Jaymar Studios, Belfast, has been instrumental in widening the choice of material at my disposal by making available many items of great interest hitherto unpublished because of poor quality.

Finally, though primarily a sequence of pictorial essays, a selection of photographs such as this assumes full meaning only when each item is coupled with relevant and interesting information and in the assembly of this from a wide range of sources the services of the late Mr T. J. Maguire and his staff in the Stationery Office, and of the typists at Fermanagh House, have been invaluable.

The author is grateful to the following for permission to reproduce illustrations in Volume 2: Alfred Montgomery, 7, 8 (bottom); Walter McGrath, 8 (top), 56, 59 (top), 101; Father P. Cusack SJ, 50 (top), 85 (bottom), 88 (bottom); A. Guinness Son & Co Ltd, 9, 10, 11; Maurice Batley, 12 (bottom), 90 (bottom); R. N. Clements, 13 (both pictures), 37 (bottom), 45 (bottom), 54 (bottom), 55 (bottom), 58 (top), 60, 66 (bottom), 81, 85 (top), 87, 102 (top); J. H. Houston, 12 (top), 15, 23 (top), 63 (top), 69 (both pictures), 83 (bottom); National Library of Ireland, 16 (bottom), 17, 18 (top), 21, 22 (bottom), 35 (both pictures), 37 (top), 38 (both pictures), 42 (both pictures), 74 (bottom); William Robb, 18 (bottom), 23 (bottom), 25, 30, 49, 50 (bottom), 51, 52, 55 (top), 59 (bottom), 77, 80 (bottom); H. C. Casserley, 19 (top), 67, 68 (bottom), 96 (top); G. R. Mahon, 40 (top); Duffner Bros, Dundalk, 22 (top), 32, 75, 80 (top); Ulster Folk Museum, 24 (bottom); Drew Donaldson, 26; Irish News, 27 (top); J. D. FitzGerald, 46, 47; Irish Railway Record Society, 28 (top), 40 (bottom), 43 (top), 57, 62, 71, 72; Ulster Museum, 28 (bottom), 39 (both pictures), 48 (top), 53, 63 (bottom), 64 (both pictures), 65 (bottom), 70 (top), 74 (top), 78; the late J. Macartney Robbins, 29 (bottom); Public Record Office Northern Ireland, 33, 73 (both pictures); Ulster Journal of Archaeology, 34 (both figures); Ministry of Finance Northern Ireland, 36 (top), 41, 90 (top), 91 (all three pictures), 95 (bottom), 98 (both pictures); Transport Museum, Belfast, 36 (bottom), 103 (both pictures), 104 (both pictures); Mrs L. Bretland, Malahide, 65 (top); Ian Allan Ltd, 16 (top), 20; Armagh County Museum, 68 (top); Belfast Telegraph, 88 (top); CIE, 70 (centre and bottom pictures); Dr E. M. Patterson, 48 (bottom); Irish Independent, 76; Deegan Photo Ltd, Dublin, 66 (top), 93 (top), 96 (bottom), 102 (bottom); NIR, 79, 82 (top); Irish Times, 84 (top); Roger Weatherup, 84 (bottom), 97; Central Library, Belfast, 82 (bottom), 83 (top); Tony O'Malley Pictures Ltd, Dublin, 93 (bottom); R. Clements Lyttle, Belfast, 61, 86, 94, 95 (top); P. McKeown, 58 (bottom); Allison Studios, Armagh, 43 (bottom), 89 (bottom); Lance King, 99; Noel Craig, 45 (top); Locomotive & General Railway Photographs, 44.

BIBLIOGRAPHY

In addition to a wide range of miscellaneous manuscript and printed company material in Dublin, Belfast and London, the following sources were consulted. Unless otherwise stated the place of publication is London.

AHRONS, E. L. *The British Steam Railway Locomotive from 1825 to 1925.* (1927)
AHRONS, E. L. *Locomotive & Train Working in the latter part of the Nineteenth Century, Vol 6.* (Cambridge, 1954)
ANDREWS, J. H. 'Road Planning in Ireland before the Railway Age', *Irish Geography*, Vol 5 No 1 (1964), 17-41
Annual Reports of the Commissioners of Public Works in Ireland, 1833-
Appendix to the Final Report of the Vice-Regal Commission on Irish Railways, H.C. 1910 [Cd 5248]

APPLETON, J. H. *The Geography of Communications in Great Britain.* (Oxford, 1962)
ARNOLD, R. M. *Steam over Belfast Lough* (Lingfield, Surrey, 1969)
Atlas to accompany the Second Report of the Railway Commissioners, 1838. (Dublin and London, 1838)
BARRIE, D. S. M. *The Dundalk Newry & Greenore Railway.* (Lingfield, Surrey, 1957)
Belfast & Northern Counties Railway : Tourist Guides. (Belfast, 1901)
BELL, A. M. *Locomotives*, 2 vols. (1936)
BENN, G. *A History of Belfast*, 2 vols. (Belfast and London, 1877-80)
BIANCONI, M. O'C., & WATSON, S. J. *Bianconi, King of the Irish Roads.* (1962)
BOOCOCK, C. P. *Irish Railway Album.* (1968)
BULLEID, H. A. V. *The Aspinall Era.* (1968)
Bulletin of the Irish Railway Society ('Fayle's Bulletin')
BUTT, J. *The Industrial Archaeology of Scotland.* (Newton Abbot, 1968)
CADFRYN-ROBERTS, J. (ed) *Coaches and Trains.* (1965)
CARTER, E. F. *An Historical Geography of the Railways of the British Isles.* (1959)
CASSERLEY, H. C. *The Historic Locomotive Pocketbook.* (1960)
CLAPHAM, J. H. *An Economic History of Modern Britain : the early railway age, 1820-1850.* (Cambridge, 1926)
CLEMENTS, R. N., & ROBBINS, J. M. *The A.B.C. of Irish Locomotives.* (1949)
COAKHAM, D. G. 'LMS (NCC) Narrow gauge coaches 1', *Model Railway News*, No 40 (1964), 608-13
COLE, D. *Irish Industrial & Contractors' Locomotives.* (1962)
CONROY, J. C. *A History of Railways in Ireland.* (1928)
COX, R. C. (ed) *The School of Engineering, Trinity College Dublin : a Record of Past and Present Students, 1841-1966.* (Dublin, 1967)
CREEDON, C. *The Cork & Macroom Direct Railway.* (Cork, 1960)
CURRAN, R. G. *A Geographical Appreciation of the Narrow Gauge Railways of County Antrim*, undergraduate dissertation (typescript), 1959, Geography Dept, Queen's University, Belfast
D'ALTON, J. *A History of Drogheda.* (Dublin, 1844)
DELANY, V. T. H. & D. R. *The Canals of the South of Ireland.* (Newton Abbot, 1967)
DUCKWORTH, C. L. D., & LANGMUIR, G. E. *Railway and Other Steamers.* (Newton Abbot, 1968)
FAYLE, H. *Narrow Gauge Railways of Ireland.* (1946)
FAYLE, H., & NEWHAM, A. T. *The Dublin & Blessington Steam Tramway.* (Lingfield, Surrey, 1962)
FAYLE, H., & NEWHAM, A. T. *The Waterford & Tramore Railway.* (Dawlish, 1964)
Final Report of the Vice-Regal Commission on Irish Railways, H.C. 1910 [Cd 5247] XXXVII 1
First Report of the Royal Commission on Irish Public Works, H.C. 1887 [C 5038] XXV 471
FISHER, C. A. 'Evolution of the Irish Railway System' in *Economic Geography*, 17 (1941), 262-74
FLANAGAN, P. J. *The Cavan & Leitrim Railway.* (Newton Abbot, 1966)
FLANAGAN, P. J. (ed) *The '101' class locomotives of the Great Southern & Western Railway.* (Dublin, 1966)
FLANAGAN, P. J. *Transport in Ireland, 1880-1910.* (Dublin, 1969)
FREEMAN, T. W. *Ireland : its physical, historical, social and economic geography.* (1950)
FREEMAN, T. W. *Pre-Famine Ireland.* (Manchester, 1957)
GAMBLE, B. *A Lecture on Transport by Rail.* (Belfast, 1919)
GEOGHEGAN, S. 'A Description of the Tramways and Rolling Stock at Guinness' Brewery', *Proc Inst Mechanical Engineers.* (1888), 327-62
GLASGOW, H. L. *The Upper Bann Navigation Rate.* (Cookstown, 1916)
GREEN, C. F. 'On Light Railways, or remunerative railways, for thinly populated districts', *Trans of the Inst Civil Engineers, Ireland*, Vol XIII (1881), 158-226
GREEN, E. R. R. *The Lagan Valley 1800-1850.* (1949)
GREEN, E. R. R. *The Industrial Archaeology of County Down.* (Belfast, HMSO, 1963)
HADFIELD, E. C. R. *Atmospheric Railways : a Victorian venture in silent speed.* (Newton Abbot, 1967)
HERRING, I. J. 'Ulster Roads on the Eve of the Railway Age', *Irish Historical Studies*, Vol II (1941-2), 160-88
HESLINGA, M. W. *The Irish Border as a Cultural Divide.* (Amsterdam, 1962)
HUTCHISON, W. R. *Tyrone Precinct.* (Belfast, 1951)
ILLINGWORTH, T. *Battery Traction on Tramways and Railways.* (Lingfield, Surrey, 1961)
Illustrated London News
Irish Railway Charts. (Dublin, 1854)
JONES, E. *A Social Geography of Belfast.* (Oxford, 1960)
Journals of the Irish Railway Record Society

Journals of the Stephenson Locomotive Society
KANE, Sir R. *The Industrial Resources of Ireland.* (Dublin, 1845)
KIDNER, R. W. *The Narrow Gauge Railways of Ireland.* (Lingfield, Surrey, 1960)
LARDNER, Rev D. *The Steam Engine.* (1836)
LEE, J. 'The Provision of Capital for Early Irish Railways', *Irish Historical Studies*, Vol XVI, No 61 (March 1968), 33-63
LEE, J. 'The Construction Costs of Irish Railways', *Business History*, No 9 (1967), 95-109
LEWIN, H. G. *Early British Railways.* (1925)
LEWIS, W. 'Narrow Gauge Railways, Ireland', *Trans of the Inst Civil Engineers, Ireland*, Vol XIII (1881), 122-57
LIDDLE, L. H. *Steam Finale.* (1964)
Locomotive Magazine
McCONNELL, R. J. *The Narrow Gauge Railways of County Donegal*, undergraduate dissertation (typescript), 1961, Geography Dept, Queen's University, Belfast
McCUTCHEON, W. A. *The Development and Decline of Inland Waterways and Standard Gauge Railways in the North of Ireland.* Unpublished PhD thesis in the library of the Queen's University, Belfast (1962)
McCUTCHEON, W. A. 'Ulster Railway Engineering and Architecture', *Ulster Journal of Archaeology*, Vol 27 (1964), 155-65
McCUTCHEON, W. A. *The Canals of the North of Ireland.* (Dawlish, 1965)
McGRATH, W. *Some Industrial Railways of Ireland.* (Cork, 1959)
McGRATH, W. 'Cork Blackrock & Passage Railway', *Cuisle na Tire* (CIE Journal), (June 1950)
McGRATH, W. 'Cork & Youghal Railway', *Cuisle na Tire* (CIE Journal), (July 1950)
McGRATH, W. 'Cork & Muskerry Light Railway', *Cork Evening Echo* (29 December 1954)
McGRATH, W. 'Cork Bandon & South Coast Railway', *Southern Star* (Skibbereen), (Sept/Oct 1951)
McGRATH, W. 'Listowel & Ballybunion Railway', *Cork Weekly Examiner* (27 January 1951)
McGRATH, W. 'Tralee & Dingle Light Railway', *Cork Evening Echo* (18 May 1951 and 27 May 1953)
McGRATH, W. 'West Clare Railway', *Cork Weekly Examiner* (April 1953)
McGRATH, W. 'Schull & Skibbereen Light Railway', *Cork Holly Bough* (Christmas 1952)
McGUIGAN, J. H. *The Giant's Causeway Tramway.* (Lingfield, Surrey, 1964)
McNEILL, D. B. *Ulster Tramways and Light Railways.* (Belfast, 1956)
McNEILL, D. B. 'The Little Railway Mania in County Antrim', *Ulster Journal of Archaeology*, Vol 16 (1953), 85-92
McNEILL, D. B. *Coastal Passenger Steamers and Inland Navigations in the North of Ireland.* (Belfast, 1960)
McNEILL, D. B. *Coastal Passenger Steamers and Inland Navigations in the South of Ireland.* (Belfast, 1965)
MACDEVITT, E. O. *A Manual of the Acts for the Construction of Tramways and Light Railways in Ireland.* (Dublin, 1883)
MARSHALL, W. S. *The Operating Department of the LMS (NCC) in War Time, 1939-45.* (Belfast, 1946)
MEASOM, G. S. *Illustrated Guide to the Midland Great Western Railway, the Dublin & Drogheda Railway and the Great Southern & Western Railway.* (1866)
MORTON, R. G. *Standard Gauge Railways in the North of Ireland.* (Belfast, 1962)
MULLINS, M. B. 'An Historical Sketch of Engineering in Ireland', *Trans of the Inst Civil Engineers, Ireland*, Vol VI (1859-61), 1-181
MURLAND, J. W. 'Observations on Irish Railway Statistics', *Trans of the Dublin Statistical Society.* (Dublin, 1849)
MURRAY, K. A. *The Great Northern Railway (Ireland).* (Dublin, 1944)
NEWHAM, A. T. *The Dublin & Lucan Tramway.* (Lingfield, Surrey, 1961)
NEWHAM, A. T. *The Schull & Skibbereen Tramway.* (Lingfield, Surrey, 1964)
NEWHAM, A. T. *The Listowel & Ballybunion Railway.* (Lingfield, Surrey, 1966)
NEWHAM, A. T. *The Cork & Muskerry Light Railway.* (Lingfield, Surrey, 1967)
NEWHAM, A. T. *The Cork Blackrock & Passage Railway.* (Lingfield, Surrey, 1968)
Northern Ireland Railways—Report by Henry Benson. Govt of N. Ireland, Cmd 458 (1963)
Northern Counties Committee, *Centenary Booklet of the Belfast & Ballymena Railway.* (Belfast, 1948)
O'CONNELL, M. J. *Charles Bianconi, 1786-1875.* (1878)
O'DELL, A. C. *Railways and Geography.* (1956)
PATTERSON, F. M. *The Belfast & County Down Railway.* (Lingfield, Surrey, 1958)
PATTERSON, F. M. *The Great Northern Railway of Ireland.* (Lingfield, Surrey, 1962)

PATTERSON, E. M. *The County Donegal Railways—A History of the Narrow Gauge Railways of North West Ireland—Part One.* (Dawlish, 1962)
PATTERSON, E. M. *The Lough Swilly Railway—A History of the Narrow Gauge Railways of North West Ireland—Part Two.* (Dawlish, 1964)
PATTERSON, E. M. *The Ballycastle Railway—A History of the Narrow Gauge Railways of North East Ireland—Part One.* (Dawlish, 1965)
PATTERSON, E. M. *The Ballymena Lines—A History of the Narrow Gauge Railways of North East Ireland—Part Two.* (Newton Abbot, 1968)
PEARSALL, A. W. H. *North Irish Channel Services.* (Belfast, 1961)
PENDER, B., & RICHARDS, H. *Irish Railways Today.* (Dublin, 1967)
Plan proposed by Sir James C. Anderson and Jasper W. Rogers for establishing Steam Carriages for the Conveyance of Goods and Passengers on the Mail Coach Roads of Ireland. (Dublin, 1841)
PORTER, J. G. V. *Mistakes of the Dundalk & Enniskillen Railway Company's Directors and their Consequences to the Shareholders, to the County Fermanagh and to the Province of Ulster.* (pamphlet). (Dublin, 1859)
PRICE, A. 'The Location, Construction and Equipment of light or secondary railways', *Trans of the Inst Civil Engineers, Ireland*, Vol XXV (1894), 93-107
Public Transport in Northern Ireland—Reports of the Commissioner holding the Public Inquiry and of the Committee of Inquiry. Govt of N Ireland, Cmd 198 (1938)
Public Transport in Northern Ireland. Govt of N Ireland, Cmd 232 (1946)
Railway Magazine
Railway Progress 1909-1959. 2 vols (to mark the Jubilee of the Stephenson Locomotive Society) (1959)
RANSOME-WALLIS, P. *Train Ferries of the World.* (1968)
Report of the Commissioners appointed to inspect the accounts and examine the works of Railways in Ireland. H.C. 1867-8 [4018] XXXII 469
Report of the Committee appointed to inquire into the Board of Works Ireland. H.C. 1878 [C 2060] XXIII 1
Report of the Railway Commission in Northern Ireland. Govt of N Ireland, Cmd 10 (1922)
Report from the Joint Select Committee on Road and Rail Transport in Northern Ireland. Govt of N Ireland, H.C. No 472 (June, 1939)
Return of the various charges made by existing railway companies for the carriage of passengers, cattle, coal and various kinds of merchandise. H.C. 1845 (614) XXXIX 22
ROBINSON, Prof A. H. 'The 1837 maps of Henry Drury Harness', *Geographical Journal*, Vol CXXI, Pt 4 (December 1955), 440-50
ROGERS, Col H. C. B. *Turnpike to Iron Road.* (1961)
ROLT, L. T. C. *Red for Danger.* (1955)
SCALLY, J. K. *The Economic Geography of the Iron Ores and Bauxites of County Antrim,* unpublished MSc thesis in the library of the Queen's University, Belfast (1954)
SCRUTATOR. *Some Considerations in Proof of the Superiority of the Packet Route via Larne and Stranraer contrasted with that via Donaghadee and Portpatrick.* (pamphlet). (Larne, 1862)
Second Report of the Commissioners appointed to consider and recommend a general system of Railways for Ireland. H.C. 1837-8 (145) XXXV 449
Second Report of the Tidal Harbours Commission. H.C. 1846 [692] XVIII 1
Second Report of the Royal Commission on Irish Public Works. H.C. 1888 [C 5264] XLVIII 143
SHEPHERD, W. E. *Twentieth Century Irish Locomotives.* (1966)
SIMMONS, J. *Transport* in series entitled *A Visual History of Modern Britain.* (1962)
SIMMONS, J. *Transport Museums.* (1970)
SNELL, J. B. *Early Railways.* (1964)
SPRINKS, N. W. *The Sligo Leitrim & Northern Counties Railway.* (London, IRRS, 1970)
TATLOW, J. *50 years of railway life.* (Reprinted from the *Railway Gazette*, 1920)
The British Railway Locomotive, 1803-1853. (London, HMSO, 1958)
Transport Conditions in Northern Ireland. Govt of N Ireland, Cmd 160 (1934)
Ulster Railway Handbook. (Belfast, 1848)
WATSON, R. A. 'The Iron Mines of Antrim', *Dublin University Magazine*, January 1874, 1-14
WHISHAW, F. *The Railways of Great Britain and Ireland.* (1840)
WHITEHOUSE, P. B. *Narrow Gauge Album.* (1957)
WHITEHOUSE, P. B. *The Tralee & Dingle Railway.* (1958)
WINCHESTER, C. (ed) *Railway Wonders of the World.* 2 vols (1936)

INDEX

Achill, 31
Adavoyle, 84
Adelaide, 90, 97
AEC rail-car sets, 94
AEC road 'bus, 69
Air-raid damage, 82
Aldergrove, 83
Alexandra, Queen, 53
American ambassador's train, 87
'American Mails', 14, 17
Amiens St Station, 38, 74, 87
Annalong, 8
Antrim, 83
Antrim, 58
Ardnacrusha, 8
Ards Circuit, 55
Ards Peninsula, 22, 69
Armagh, 89
Armour plated locomotive, 56, 57
Armoured rail cars, 56
Arrow, 16, 58
Athenry, 16
Athlone, 16, 54, 68, 85
Atock, Martin, 16
Automatic crossing gates, 98
Avonside Engine Co, 8, 9

Ballaghaderreen branch, 16
Ballinascarthy, 101
Ballyards viaduct, 72
Ballycastle Railway, 23, 50
Ballygeary, 19
Ballymacarrett Junction, 29, 39
Ballymena, 23, 63, 80
Ballymena & Larne Railway, 23
Ballymoney, 50
Balmoral, 59
'Baltic' tanks, 45
Bangor, 14, 22, 25, 29, 45, 74, 98
Barclay, Andrew, 7
Bazin, J. R., 50, 87
Belfast, 10, 14, 22, 23, 24, 26, 27, 28, 29, 30, 38, 46, 49, 52, 59, 62, 63, 65, 66, 74, 78, 80, 82, 86, 87, 90, 92, 95, 98, 100, 103, 104
Belfast Central Railway, 25, 27, 103
Belfast Corporation, 100
Belfast & County Down Railway, 22, 25, 27, 29, 38, 39, 45, 53, 55, 62, 69, 74, 88, 103
Belfast & Northern Counties Railway, 12, 15, 18, 24, 35, 36, 50, 62, 64, 69
Beyer Peacock & Co, 18, 30, 45, 49, 50, 51, 52, 55, 58, 63, 84
Blackrock, 27
Blanche, 103
Bleach Green viaducts, 73
Bo-Bo wheel formation, 93
Bord na Mona, 13
Boyne, 84, 97
Boyne viaduct, 51, 78
Bray, 26, 27, 76, 93
Bray Head, 73
Bredin, E. C., 81
Breen Bridge, 73
Bretland, A. W., 62, 65
British Aluminium Company, 12
Broadstone, 16, 44, 54, 57, 60, 70, 85
Bulleid, O. V. S., 44, 96
Buncrana, 14
Bundoran, 58
'Bundoran Express', 58
Bundoran Junction, 58

Burrowing junction, 79
Burtonport, 48
Bury Curtis & Kennedy, 102

Carnlough limestone railway, 7
Carrantuohill, 49
Carrickmines, 26
Cashel, 55
Castleblayney Keady & Armagh Railway, 43, 72
Castlerock, 23
Cavan, 82
Civil War, 56, 57
Claremorris, 60
Clayton steam rail-car, 68
Clifden, 16, 31, 40
Clifford, Charles, 46, 49, 74
Clogher Valley bogie, 68
Clones, 58, 82
Clonsast, 13
Co-Co wheel formation, 93
Cobh, 14, 17, 35
Coey, Robert, 46
Cohen, George & Sons Ltd, 8
Coleraine, 23, 69
Comber, 55
Comhlucht Siuicre Eireann, 13, 49
Compound locomotives, 15, 49, 50, 51, 78, 84
Concrete, use of, 31, 79
Connemara, 16
Conner, James, 48
Connolly Station, 36, 100
Coras Iompair Eireann, 44, 58, 60, 66, 71, 85, 87, 90, 93, 95, 96, 97, 100, 101, 102
Cork, 14, 19, 26, 28, 46, 56, 60, 68, 81, 87, 92, 96, 100
Cork & Macroom Direct Railway, 68
Cork Industrial Fair & Exhibition, 59
Corrib viaduct, Galway, 40
County Antrim, 23
County Donegal Railways Joint Committee, 75
Courtaulds Ltd, 12
Courtmacsherry, 101
Courtney, 8
Craigmore viaduct, 86
Crossley diesel engine, 93
Cusack, Edward, 44
Cushina, 13
Customs examination, 51, 58, 82, 86
Cyclops, 74

Dalkey, 27
Dargan, William, 66
Dawson, John S., 65, 67
Derby, 18, 52, 61, 63
Derg, Lough, 58
Derry Road, 65, 73, 75
Diesel-hydraulic locomotive, 95
Diesel-electric locomotives, 92, 93, 94, 95
Diesel-electric trains, 93, 94, 95
Donegal, 75
Donegal town, 54
Donegall Quay, 103
Downhill tunnels, 23
Drewry petrol rail-car, 76
Drogheda, 51, 58, 78
Drumm Battery Train, 76
Drung Hill tunnel, 42
Dublin, 9, 10, 11, 14, 17, 22, 25, 26, 28, 36, 38, 46, 49, 54, 55, 58, 60, 63, 65, 74, 76, 78, 81, 85, 86, 90, 92, 93, 98, 100
Dublin & Kingstown Railway, 27
Dublin & South Eastern Railway, 93

110

Dublin & Wicklow Railway, 26
Dundalk, 33, 49, 58, 63, 65, 75, 77, 80, 82, 84, 100, 102
Dundalk Newry & Greenore Railway, 77
Dundrum, 26
Dunmurry, 95
Dun Laoghaire, 14, 92
Dunluce Castle, 45
Dunseverick Castle, 45

Eagle, 51, 86, 95
Earl of Ulster, 61
Edenderry, 58, 85
Edward VII, 53, 70
Elizabeth II, 61
English Electric, 95
'Enterprise Express', 51, 86
    ,,   Dublin-Belfast, 86, 95
    ,,   Dublin-Cork, 87
Ennis, 66, 100
Enniskillen, 37, 58, 91
Erin's Isle, 22
ESB, 13
Eucharistic Congress (1932), 58

Fair Special, 54
Fairy, 62
Falcon, 51, 95
Fortwilliam Sidings, 99
Foxrock, 26
Foyle viaduct, Lifford, 41

Gaelic Athletic Association, 58
    ,,   special, 85
Galway, 16, 40, 92
General Motors diesel-electrics, 93
Geoghegan locomotives, 9-11
George VI, 59
Glenties, 13
Glover, G. T., 49, 51, 84, 95
Glynn, 18
Gobbins, The, 24
'Golfers' Express', 80
Goraghwood, 82, 102
Gortnagallon, 83
Great Northern Railway Board, 97
Great Northern Railway (Ireland), 22, 25, 27, 29, 30, 31, 32, 33, 34, 38, 46, 49, 51, 59, 61, 62, 63, 65, 70, 73, 74, 75, 77, 80, 82, 83, 84, 85, 86, 89, 94, 95, 103
Great Southern Railways, 8, 55, 62, 65, 68, 76, 81
Great Southern & Western Railway, 9, 17, 20, 21, 29, 31, 46, 62, 70, 102
Great Victoria St Station, Belfast, 29, 49, 51, 94, 95
Greenisland, 79
Guinness, Arthur Son & Co Ltd, 9-11

Harcourt St Station, 26
Harland & Wolff, 49, 83
Haulage waggon/bogie, 10, 11
Heuston Station, 100
Hill of Down, 54
Hill of Howth Tramway, 22
Holden Train, 15
Holywood Arches, 38
Horse tramways, 27
Howden, G. B., 77, 78
Howden-Meredith wheel, 77
Howth, 22, 63
Hudswell Clarke, 48
Hydraulic hoist, 10
Hydro electricity, 8

Inchicore, 17, 20, 26, 28, 44, 46, 50, 55, 62, 66, 70, 80, 81, 84, 85, 87, 96, 100, 101, 102, 104
Industrial archaeology, 100
Industrial railways, 7-13

Inny, 58
Inspection trolley, 64
    ,,   car, 64
Irish Free State Army Railway Repair & Maintenance Corps, 56, 57
Irish Railway Record Society, 100, 101, 103
Irish Republican Army, 89
Islandmagee, 24

'J15', 26, 28, 102
'Jeep', 45, 52, 90, 99

Keady, 31, 43
Kent Station (Glanmire Rd), Cork, 102
Kestrel, 51
Killarney, 21
'Killarney Express', 20
Killary Harbour, 16
Killeshandra, 58
Killiney, 27, 93
Killyhevlin viaduct (Weir's Bridge), 37
King Edward VII, 15
Kingsbridge Station, 9, 10, 20, 96
Kitson & Co, 23
Knock, 60
Knockmore Junction, 83
Knock pilgrimage traffic, 60

Lagan Bridge, 25, 103
Lagan valley, 30
Larne, 22, 24
Larne Harbour, 12, 14, 18, 23, 52
Leixlip, 58
Lifford, 41
Limavady, 91
Limerick, 8, 58
Limerick Junction, 87, 92
Lime-washed waggons, 54
'Limited Mails', 49, 65, 74
Lisahally, 61
Lisburn, 15, 30, 61, 63, 98
Livestock special, 54
Locomotive interchange, 46, 47
London Midland & Scottish Railway (Northern Counties Committee), 23, 31, 45, 52, 61, 78, 80, 82, 83, 84
Londonderry, 14, 23, 36, 78, 91, 92, 95, 104
Londonderry & Coleraine Railway, 23
Londonderry & Lough Swilly Railway, 48
Londonderry Port & Harbour Commissioners, 104
Londonderry steam road waggon, 69
Longpavement, 8
Loop line, 78, 79, 80
Lurgan, 15

Macha, 81
Maeve, 81, 104
Magheramorne, 52, 99
Malcolm, Bowman, 15, 45, 50
Mallow, 13, 21, 87, 100, 101
Maysfields, 103
McDonnell, Alexander, 17, 62, 101
McIntosh, H. R., 80, 84
Metropolitan Carriage & Waggon Co, 68
Metropolitan Vickers Electrical Co Ltd, 93
Mercuric, 44
Merlin, 51, 95
Midland Great Western Railway, 16, 31, 40, 44, 54, 57, 58, 60, 65, 66, 67, 68, 70, 75, 85
Midland Railway, 18
Midland Railway (Northern Counties Committee), 15, 23, 31, 63
Mills, W. H., 32, 33
Miniature railway, 59
Ministry of Finance (NI), 100
Mogul engines, 52, 60, 61, 80, 83

III

Monaghan, 82, 89
Monkstown, 78, 79
Morris of Loughborough, 65
Morton, W. H., 44
Motor trains (BCDR), 29
Motor trains (GN), 30
Motorways, 92
Mount, 12
Mountjoy, 90
Mourne Bridge, Strabane, 73
Mourne Mountains, 8
Mullingar, 16, 54, 57, 88
Mussenden Temple, 23
Mystery Train, 55

Nasmyth Wilson & Co, 29, 30
National Institute for Physical Planning, 100
Neilson Reid, 74
Neptune, 46
Newport tunnel, 42
'North Atlantic Express', 80
North British Locomotive Co, 45, 46
North Wall, Dublin, 96
Northern Ireland Railways, 71, 92, 95, 98, 99, 100

O'Briensbridge, 8
Oil-burning locomotives, 85
'Orange' special, 54
Orenstein & Koppel, 13
Otter, 7
Oughterard, 16

Parking meters, 92
Parkmore, 24
Pay carriage, 62
Pearson, S. & Co Ltd, 8
Peckett & Sons Ltd, 12
Pettigo, 58
Peregrine, 51
Pilgrimage specials, 58, 60
Pilot, 57
'Pioneer' special, 58
Portadown, 15, 29, 71, 75
Portarlington, 13, 50, 85
Portrush, 22, 35, 69, 80, 92
'Portrush Flyer', 80
Public Record Office Northern Ireland, 100
Push-and-pull trains (BCDR), 29
Push-and-pull trains (GN), 30, 63

Queen's Bridge, 103
Queen's Quay, 25, 29, 39, 45, 88
Queenstown (Cobh), 14, 17, 35

Radio Train, 60
Rail 'buses, 69, 75, 77
Rail-cars (GN), 75
Rail closures, 88, 89
Rail motors (GN), 30
Railway Preservation Society of Ireland, 49, 59, 100, 101, 102, 103
Rosslare, 14, 19, 27, 31, 40, 92
Royal saloon (BCDR), 53
Royal saloon (GN), 70
Royal train (UTA), 61
Royal visits, 38, 53, 59, 61

Seaham Harbour Engine Works, 69
Seahill Halt, 98
Shankill, 26
Shannon, 8
Shoppers' special, 82
Signals and signal cabins, 39, 45
Siemens Bauunion, 8
Silent Valley, 8

Sion Mills, 33, 34
Skew bridge, 90
Slieve Gullion, 49, 59
Sligo, 68, 92
Sligo Leitrim & Northern Counties Railway, 37, 44, 52
Spence, William, 9, 10
'Spoil' trains, 52, 92, 99
Sprite, 62
State carriage, 66
Steam carriages, 62, 63
Steam rail-cars (GN), 63
Stephenson, Robert & Co, 104
Stillorgan, 26
Strabane, 73, 82
Strabane & Letterkenny Railway, 41
Straffan, 81
Suir viaduct, 40
Sutton, 22

Tailte, 81
Tassagh viaduct, 43
Terrorist attacks, 89
The Braid, 80
Thomastown, 37
Thurles, 13
Tiger, 85
Timoleague & Courtmacsherry Railway, 101
Tivoli, 28
'Tourist Train', 16
Tourist Trophy Motor Car Race, 55
Track layer, 65
Track lifting, 75, 89
Tralee, 21
Transport Museums, 9, 10, 62, 66, 100, 103, 104
Travelling Post Office, 65
Tuam, 13
Tullyaughter, 7
Turf burner, 96
Turf train, 85
Twelve Pins, 16
Tynan, 82

Ulster Folk Museum, 100, 103
Ulster Junction, 27
Ulster Transport Authority, 75, 84, 88, 89, 90, 95, 97
Ulster Transport Authority Royal train, 61
Ulster Transport Museum, 10, 45, 51, 62, 66, 81, 100, 103, 104
Unemployment relief scheme, 79

Valentia Harbour branch, 31
Valentine's Glen, 79
Victoria Bridge, 73
Victoria Park Halt, 29
Victoria Road, Londonderry, 91

Waterford, 19, 31, 40, 67, 92
Waterford & Kilkenny Railway, 37
Waterford & Tramore Railway, 68
Waterford & Tramore coupé, 67
Waterside, Londonderry, 36
Watson, E. A., 87
Weir's Bridge (Killyhevlin), 37
West Clare saloon, 66
Westport, 16
Wexford, 100
Whiteabbey, 45, 73, 78
Whitehead, 24, 64, 99, 100, 102
Wicklow, 76
Wilfrid, 12
Withdrawal of services, 88, 89
Woolwich Mogul, 60, 88

York Road, 15, 18, 23, 36, 45, 50, 61, 64, 80, 82, 92, 102
Youghal, 14, 19, 28